BE THE HERO

Be the Change

Matthew S. Friedman

TABLE OF CONTENTS

Part One:
The Problem

1

MY PERSONAL JOURNEY

For the past 35 years, I have been fighting human trafficking. My exposure to this topic happened as a result of my work with the United States Agency for International Development (USAID) in Nepal. I was a public health officer assigned to manage a national HIV/AIDS program. This work brought me face-to-face with many women and girls who were forced into prostitution – something that had a devastating impact on my life. Through the other jobs that followed in Bangladesh, Thailand and Hong Kong, my experience and understanding of this topic continued to grow.

While I wish I could say I was one of those 15-year-old high school students who had a strong desire to be an activist from an early age, the reality was just the opposite. I didn't want to have anything to do with fighting any cause. Like so many, my hope and dream was to make a lot of money, live a good life and seek the happiness that I felt was my right.

But somehow, my life seemed to conspire against this outcome. To understand what happened to me, let me offer a few typical stories of victims of human trafficking I met and got to know. Stories such as the one below helped initiate a radical change in me:

"I was only 14 years old when I was sold to the brothel. I was so young; I didn't know anything. I was innocent then. My parents were tricked by a neighbor into thinking I'd be

working at a restaurant as a waitress in the city. I wanted to go. I wanted to help my family. I was willing to work. But this is not what followed. After walking through the jungle and crossing the border on a night boat, a van took me to a bad place – a place where girls like me were sold like animals to the owner. When they told me what I was supposed to do with men, I said no, never. I fought back.

That didn't stop them. They raped me and tortured me for days until I had nothing left to give. I no longer had control of my life or my body. I belonged to them. Every night I was with up to ten different men – 7 days a week, 365 days a year. For years, this was my life. Now at 18, my body is frail from the illnesses. I feel completely empty inside."

This is a typical human trafficking story. It sounds shocking, but even more appalling is the fact that 4.8 million women and girls in the world today – right now – share similar stories. They are forced to have sex with strange men every day. Few things in life are more degrading than suffering this fate.

But human trafficking goes far beyond women and girls who are forced into prostitution. Men and boys are also deceived or seduced into opportunities that do not exist; instead, they become slaves. Over the years, I encountered many other examples of modern slavery. Below are two other common scenarios:

"I was only 16 years old when I was forced on to that fishing boat. I was told that the job was easy and that I'd be paid a good wage. But instead, I ended up working 18 hours a day, every day. For food, we ate nothing but fish and rice twice a day. If I got sick or injured, I worked. I had seen others who had fallen ill and the captain simply threw them over the side

of the boat. I still remember their pleas for help as the ocean carried them away to their deaths. I was beaten if I didn't work hard enough, or even if I did.

Days often went by with only a few hours of sleep. I was so tired sometimes I felt I'd go crazy. To keep me working, they would force me to take powerful drugs that destroyed my body. When I finally returned to port after four years at sea, I was not given any pay. The captain told me that I was an illegal migrant so he didn't have to give me anything. Having no way to communicate with my family while I was away, my mother and father assumed I was dead. Since they moved away, I don't know where to find them."

Male Cambodian victim exploited in Thailand

"When I arrived at the construction site, I was so excited. The foreman told me that I could get a good job. While he said he couldn't pay me for the first three months, I didn't mind. He seemed like a respectable person. Every day I worked from 7am to 7pm. The work was hard and dangerous, but that was OK. After three months I went to get my pay. But the foreman told me that I'd have to wait another two months. While I wasn't happy, what else could I do? I borrowed more money from my friends and continued to work.

Each time I asked for my wages, I was told the same answer – next month. After 12 months passed, I was desperate. I was heavily in debt without any money. When I had heard that there were others like me, we all got together and as a group we approached the foreman. This angered him greatly. The next day, a van pulled up and the police took us all away. The foreman stood there and smiled. It was he who called them there. At that moment, I could tell that he had never intended *to pay any of us. Two weeks later, I was deported. For an entire year I worked for nothing. For an entire year, I was a slave."*

Male Laos victim exploited in Thailand

Few people would be unaffected by repeated encounters with these victims. The more I saw their pain, the more I felt it, internalized it and found myself being drawn into the response. I did not choose this issue to follow; in many ways, it chose me. I would say it consumed me – sometimes completely.

While some have said that my actions over the years have been heroic, I can't say they were ever fully intentional. I did them because I couldn't stop myself. Many times, I wish I could have walked away. My life would have been less painful. In this way, I must confess that I never really voluntarily offered my service; I was compelled to do so by a force in me that I have never been able to fully understand or control. If you have had a similar experience as an activist, you will understand this statement. Not everyone will.

The Extent of the Issue

Human trafficking, which represents the recruitment, transport, receipt and harboring of people for the purpose of exploiting their body or their labor, affects almost every part of the world. Globally, it is estimated that more than 40 million men, women and children are enslaved today. These victims, found in factories, construction sites, fisheries and sex venues, are forced to work for little or no pay, deprived of their freedom and often subjected to unimaginable suffering.

Despite our best efforts, the world is not winning the fight against human slavery. According to the US State Department's 2019 Trafficking in Persons report, it is estimated that around 100,000 victims were helped globally. Even with the collective response of governments, the United Nations and civil society partners, less than **0.2 percent** of victims are assisted annually. Relying solely on the anti-slavery community around the world to tackle the scourge of slavery and the criminals behind it simply isn't working. Unless something drastically changes, this trend will continue unabated.

Why are successful interventions so few? According to the International Labor Organization (ILO), the profits generated from this illicit criminal trade are estimated to exceed US$150 billion annually. But despite the size of the problem, annual global donor contributions add up to only some US$350 million, which represents less than one-half percent of total profits generated by traffickers. It is not surprising that the number of trafficked persons continues to increase.

In addition, the number of people working daily to combat the problem is estimated to be around 20,000. If you compare this to the 500,000 criminals estimated to be trafficking people throughout the world, you can see that the good guys are greatly outnumbered by the greed-incentivized bad guys. We have to play by the rules. They don't. They do whatever they wish to deceive, cheat, steal, beat and oppress their victims. Yes, the good guys are enormously outnumbered, but we must continue to fight.

Gita's Story: Where Were You?

The reality of the immense challenge we face in addressing the human trafficking issue came home to me years ago when I met a girl named Gita. She was a 15-year-old teenager from Nepal who was trafficked into a brothel in India and systematically raped thousands of times during a two-year period. At the time, I was living and working in Nepal, where I was researching a book on the plight of sex slaves trafficked between Nepal and India. I visited shelters for trafficking victims throughout the country.

While nearly all of the girls I approached agreed to tell me their personal stories, one girl, Gita, repeatedly declined my requests for an interview. But during all of my interviews with other girls in her shelter, she sat and listened to everything being recounted.

On the last day, Gita said she had changed her mind – she would give me an interview. Over the next three hours, she gave one of the most gut-wrenching testimonials I had ever heard. It was filled with a terrible mixture of love, life, deception, rape, torture, murder, betrayal and disease. At the end of the interview, I sat there speechless. I finally remarked, *"Wow, you must be so angry at the traffickers for all of the terrible things they did to you."*

Instead, Gita looked accusingly at me and the others in the room. *"No, I am not angry at the traffickers. I am angry at you!"* she shouted, pointing her finger at each of us in turn. *"Where were you when I was in that terrible brothel? I sat there every day waiting for someone to come and save me. I knew that everything happening around me was illegal and wrong. Where were you and everyone else when I needed you?*

"And why are you still sitting here?" she added. *"Why aren't you down there helping those other girls? Everyone knows what is going on. How can such terrible things happen without anyone doing anything? I am not angry with the traffickers. They are just bad people doing what they do – bad things. I am angry with the good people – society, you! Where were you? Why does no one care?"*

That day, a survivor spoke for herself and for so many others. She called us out, asking a fundamental question: *"Why doesn't the world care enough to stop this crime against humanity?"* It was a profoundly relevant question then and remains so today.

That moment was an epiphany that made me understand that we, the citizens of the world – collectively and individually – must take responsibility to help end the suffering of those like Gita. Slavery represents one of the most egregious human rights violations of our time. We must all accept some responsibility.

← wrong the porn connection.

So, is any one of us responsible for Gita's plight? Is there a direct relationship between the terrible things that happened to her and our own lives? The answer is a resounding "no" but who should bear the responsibility? Her parents? Her community? The police? The government? If this systematic abuse has continued for generations with little change, something must be done. Fifteen-year-old girls being commercially raped anywhere in the world is humanly unacceptable. We, as citizens of this world, must collectively take a stand. We must actively condemn this practice. How can any of us argue against this?

For me, the sense of responsibility I felt was clear. I was facing a *"wrong"* right in front of me. Over and over, a voice in my mind shouted, *"help them!"* I eventually listened. For many of us, this or other issues have a similar impact. We feel compelled to take a stand because everything in our being says we should. It is up to each of us to turn away or listen. It is a personal choice we must make.

Crossing the Line

Despite all my exposure to the world of human trafficking, I suppose, without what happened next, I might still have shaken off the things I had seen or at least obsessed less about them.

The Indian government invited me to do public health checks in the Mumbai brothels. I carried out this assignment with a police officer by my side. While other interests awaited me once this visit ended, I could not have expected the following life-changing encounter.

At one of the brothels, upon entering the waiting area, an eleven-year-old Nepalese trafficking victim saw me. She ran to me and wrapped her arms around my waist. In a local dialect that I understood, she said, *"Save me, save me, they are doing terrible things to me!"*

I looked down in shock at this young girl. She had straight black hair cut in a simple hanging style that reached to her shoulders. A dress, far too big, hung on her tiny frame. This was a child in an adult world. I can never forget the pleading desperation in her light brown eyes.

I turned to the police officer and said, *"We need to take this girl out of here now."*

"No, we can't do that," he said.

I said, *"Why not? You are a cop!"*

He replied, *"Because they will kill us before they will let us leave with her. Finding a child this age here will create a lot of problems for them."*

We left, frustrated, but returned with more policemen. Of course, the girl was gone. I will never know what happened to that precious child, but I am sure it included beatings, torture and a drastically shortened life full of misery. Almost certainly that little girl is long dead – someone so young in the brothels had a very high probability of contracting HIV and dying of AIDS.

Every once in a while, each of us is given a *"life test"*. This was mine and I failed. I should have found a way to get that girl out of that awful place and I didn't. I failed her so thoroughly that I never even learned her name.

For weeks after encountering this child, I had nightmares. I was haunted by her stricken expression and her pleading eyes looking up at me. I would wake up in a cold sweat with my heart pounding in my chest.

I also started reflecting on my own life. I had been doing public service work for years, but I finally came to realize that, to a certain extent, I had been doing this work for me – to promote Matt Friedman's career and get the next big job. It took this terrible situation to bring me back to what it was all about. It isn't about me. It's about the people out there who need help. I was humbled by this realization.

Not knowing what else to do, I finally surrendered. William Wilberforce, the great nineteenth century abolitionist, said, *"You may choose to look the other way, but you can never say again that you did not know."* I accepted that, knowing what I did about this problem, I could no longer turn away. I had to step up and become fully involved. At that moment, I became an activist. Many people who fight this injustice have a similar story to tell. The reality of the pain and suffering gets under a person's skin. Once absorbed, there is no escaping it.

In an attempt to restore some small shred of the dignity stolen from her, I call this child Amulya, which in Nepalese means "priceless". Amulya and those like her have an intrinsic worth beyond measure. To give her suffering some meaning, I tell Amulya's story in hopes that others will do what they can to protect women and girls around the world from similar fates.

Where are all the Good Men?

A few months after my encounter with Amulya, I started visiting shelters in Nepal that took in rescued trafficking victims. The best way to understand the extent of an issue is through the eyes of a person who has experienced it.

Below is a translation of a letter I received from a young girl named Jeana. She was trafficked to India and endured the brothels for several years. She had AIDS. I received her letter the day after I visited her at a shelter in Kathmandu.

The depth of Jeana's anguish can be felt in her words. Many other victims have similar thoughts and feelings that are never revealed to the world. This offers a glimpse into their broken hearts. Read these words carefully – they hold a very important message.

"Matthew,

Thank you for your kindness in coming to see me yesterday at the shelter. Your words brought great joy to my broken heart.

I turn 15 on Monday. After being used by so many men, I can see that my days will soon come to an end. My illness gets worse with each passing day. I can hardly eat. The food has no flavor. It is sour like so much of my life. I will not see my sixteenth birthday.

I look back on that day when I left my family's home. I was only 12 then. I was so happy. So full of life. I had such hopes and dreams. Now look at me. I will never marry. I will never have children. I will never have grandchildren. I will not grow old.

The day that first man took my virtue was the day my God died. He and all those other men stole my life away. I was just a child. Why did nobody come to help me? I have stopped asking why this happened to me. I have even stopped feeling angry.

I need you to promise me. I need you to do what you can to prevent any other girls from falling into this hole. Promise me you will end this evil. Promise me you will never stop trying. I don't care about myself. I'm done. Don't let any more of our sisters go through what I went through.

My spirit is already dead inside. My body will soon catch up. How can this happen to a child? Where are all the good men? Where are our protectors? Where is our humanity? Promise me.

Jeana

I read and re-read this letter at least 20 times that day, with tears streaming down my face. Many of us who work in this field are driven by these passionate pleas. This is one of so many. This young girl was only 15 years old. She was commercially raped more than 7,000 times. As we have said, there are literally millions of women and girls in this situation.

Jeana asked two important questions: *"Where are all of the good men? Where are our protectors?"* They are out there. We just need to find them, wake them up and help them to work alongside us to combat this problem.

Reading this letter so many years ago was another epiphany that helped me to understand that we, the citizens of the world – collectively and individually – have a mandate to help end the suffering of those like Jeana. Human trafficking represents one of the most disgusting human rights violations of our time.

To address this problem, I realized that we needed to establish a *"second-generation abolitionist movement"* in which we all step up and do our part. English abolitionist William Wilberforce and others led a movement more than 150 years ago. So can we. For human trafficking to end, we must care. We must all care.

What is the Point?

Human trafficking is just one of the major issues facing us today. For some, a desire to act when confronted with injustice is programmed into our DNA. For others, it needs to be encouraged and nurtured. The people who experience these violations continue to ask the world, *"Where are you? Why are you not helping us?"* It is not unreasonable for these legitimate and relevant questions to be asked.

When you read the stories above, how did they affect you? Did you feel a desire to help? Were these feelings strong enough to bring about a change? Hold on to these thoughts - we will delve deeper into this topic later in the book.

2

MAJOR ISSUES OF OUR TIME

Despite the good in the world and the progress we have made, there is still so much more to be done. Beyond the human trafficking crisis outlined previously, our world faces numerous other significant challenges. Many are catastrophic and overwhelming in their magnitude and reach. These issues manifest at all levels – global, community and interpersonal. Let's consider a few examples.

Global Problems

Climate Change: The planet is heating up. Global warming creates a slow and gradual rise in the earth's surface temperature. Temperatures today are 0.74°C (1.33°F) higher than they were 150 years ago. Many scientists say that in the next 150 years, temperatures could rise to 6°C (11°F) higher than they are now. Imagine that scenario. While the increase of a few degrees doesn't sound significant, in reality it can have a profound impact on millions of people.

Among the greenhouse gases, the concentration and increase of carbon dioxide (CO_2) in the atmosphere is the main cause of global warming. Using fossil fuels like coal and oil adds carbon dioxide to the air. When more trees are cut down (deforestation), there are fewer plants to remove carbon dioxide from the atmosphere.

As our earth gets hotter, the sea levels rise. This is because water expands when it gets warmer, and because warm temperatures melt glaciers faster than they can be replaced. The sea-level rise will cause coastal areas to disappear. For low-lying countries, this will have a horrific impact. Many communities in Miami, Florida, are already seeing this process happen every time the tide comes in. Our disappearing coastlines will render some areas uninhabitable in the future.

During a recent trip to Bangladesh, I met an academic who had this to say about climate change: *"What are we going to do when the ocean begins taking our land away? It is already happening. We have so many people and so little land. Those who will need to move will have to go inland. But where? We don't have any place for them. We are already bursting at the seams. What is theoretical for everyone else is a reality to us. What will we do?"*

Weather patterns, including where and how much rain or snow there is, also are changing because of global warming. Each year, the number and severity of hurricanes around the world continues to increase. Deserts are growing in size. Colder areas are warming up faster than warm areas. Strong storms are occurring more frequently and agriculture is suffering, leading to lower food production.

However, these effects are not irreversible. There are things we can all do to address climate change but we are not doing them fast enough. Can one individual help? Maybe not to any extent but multiply an individual's efforts by thousands or millions and perhaps we can heal our planet.

Dire Poverty: It is estimated that 1.2 billion people live on less than $1 per day and almost three billion on less than $2 per day. Imagine how hard it is for anyone to live on this tiny amount of money. On any given day, I walk into a convenience store and pay five times as much for simple snacks.

Other factors are interrelated with poverty. For example, 110 million primary school-aged children cannot afford to attend school and 60 percent of them are girls. Many of these families live without adequate food, shelter, safe water and sanitation. All of these factors directly contribute to extreme poverty and this goes beyond an individual's lack of income and resources. It is affected by economic, social, human rights and governance factors. In essence, it robs people of opportunities, choices, services and, in too many cases, hope.

What is shocking about this situation is that wealth around the world is increasingly concentrated with the top 1 percent now owning more than 50 percent of the world's wealth.

Fighting poverty is a moral imperative. In recognition of this, the international community adopted years of plans and strategies. However, progress in meeting their goals has been slow and uneven across regions. The global community needs to make a concerted effort to accelerate progress and more effectively address the causes of poverty at country and global levels.

Two memorable quotes related to poverty encapsulate this issue:

> *"Overcoming poverty is not a gesture of charity. It is the protection of a fundamental human right, the right to dignity and a decent life."*
>
> — Nelson Mandela

> *"The test of our progress is not whether we add more to the abundance of those who have much, it is whether we provide enough for those who have too little."*
>
> — Franklin D. Roosevelt

Fresh Water Scarcity: Water scarcity represents a lack of fresh, drinkable water in a given area. This issue tends to affect arid and desert areas and places where the water is too polluted to drink. Water scarcity results from both human and natural causes. Changes in climate and weather patterns can reduce the availability of water. Common human causes include over-consumption, bad governance, pollution and increases in the demand for water.

The World Bank and the United Nations have been sounding the alarm over a global water crisis for many years. A joint report released in 2017 stated that 40 percent of the world's population is now affected by water scarcity. The report goes on to say that 700 million people are at risk of being displaced by intense water scarcity by 2030. More than two billion people are compelled to drink unsafe water and more than 4.5 billion people do not have safely managed sanitation services.

When I lived in Nepal, I observed many examples of the impact of water scarcity. In some hill communities, people had to walk for two hours down to the river and two hours back to bring water to their homes each day. This burden consumed four hours that could have been used for more productive purposes. When asked what single most important change in their life would help them the most, many women said "wells". For them, not having accessible water was their biggest challenge.

There are many solutions to this issue, including educating people to change consumption and lifestyles; inventing new water conservation technologies; recycling wastewater; improving irrigation and agricultural practices and developing energy-efficient desalination plants. However, for this to happen, many more of us need to get involved.

World Hunger: On any given day, 11.3 percent of the world population goes hungry. That's more than 800 million people who don't receive adequate daily nourishment. While the world produces enough food to feed its 7.6 billion people, those who go hungry either do not have land to grow food or money to purchase it. Poverty is considered to be the principal cause of hunger.

In 2018, an estimated 8.3 million children died of hunger. Poor nutrition and too often, slow starvation, played a role in nearly half these deaths. Nearly 98 percent of worldwide hunger exists in underdeveloped countries. Almost 1 in every 15 children in developing countries dies before the age of five, most of them from hunger-related causes.

Even in developed countries, hunger can be a problem. The US Department of Agriculture (USDA) reported that 12.3 percent of American households remain "food insecure" – meaning that 1 in 8 US households had difficulty at some time during the year obtaining enough food for all their members. According to USDA, more than 41 million Americans face hunger, including nearly 13 million children. The groups experiencing the highest rates of food insecurity include households with children led by single women and people living below the poverty level.

Here is one person's description of hunger:

> "I had no idea when I'd get my next meal. Between these times, all I could think about was food. It became my only thought. As my stomach churned and ached, I would drink water to fill the emptiness I felt. I did this to fool my body into thinking it was satisfied. But this never worked for long. I felt my hunger. It became who I was. Sometimes I'd try to sleep. But when I opened my eyes, it was back. That void, that obsessive desire for food, that ache. There are few things in life more awful."

I once fasted for three full days – only drinking water. I experienced several of the emotions and physical sensations described above. I couldn't imagine how awful it would be to face this every day. In my case, it was voluntary but for millions it is a daily reality.

Lack of Education: More than 72 million of the world's school-age children are not enrolled in school. This can be attributed to a range of factors, including inequality, marginalization and poverty. Without an education, most individuals cannot find viable work that will offer a living wage. Education is the path to solving the challenges we will face in life. The more knowledge we gain, the more opportunities we have to allow us to achieve our full potential.

During my many visits to rural areas throughout Asia, I met countless uneducated children who had amazing minds and an immense appetite for knowledge. Without an education, their ability to learn, to solve problems and to reach their full potential was often lost. As the saying goes, *"a mind is a terrible thing to waste"*. Without appropriate education, this is exactly what happens.

Pollution: Global pollution is a massive problem that affects us all. Pollution takes many forms, including plastic and litter in our oceans; toxins in our air; hormones and antibiotics in our animals; fertilizers and pesticides in our soil; unsafe water and other consequences. Fresh water is an absolute necessity in our lives and yet more than one billion people do not have access to clean water. Some South Asian rivers are so polluted by toxic substances, raw sewage and industrial waste that the entire river system is completely dead.

High levels of air pollution cause an increased risk of heart attack, asthma, excessive coughing and chronic breathing problems. In Beijing, recent studies indicate that air pollution has caused lower birth rates and higher adult mortality from respiratory diseases. Lung cancer rates have gone up by over 60 percent in the past decade in China.

Even noise and light can represent forms of pollution when they occur at levels that interfere with our daily lives. Like many of the issues in this chapter, simple steps can be taken to lessen the impact of this problem.

During my five years living and working in Bangladesh, the air quality was so awful I could actually see it. There were times when I felt as if I were walking through a black cloud. The impact this had on my body was life threatening. For months at a time, if I coughed into a handkerchief, the phlegm was black. I sometimes wonder if the cancer I experienced in my life resulted from the impact of pollution on so many parts of my body.

Extinction of our Species: Many apex animals are facing possible extinction because of poaching, habitat destruction, overhunting and pollution. Some of the endangered species include tigers, cheetahs, red tuna, Asian elephants, mountain gorillas and polar bears. Unless dramatic measures are taken, our children's children will only know these creatures from pictures in history books. Like so many problems facing the world, human beings are both the cause and the potential solution.

Community Issues

Much closer to home, we can find a range of human difficulties within our own communities, including child abuse, homelessness, crime, domestic violence, bullying, inadequate emergency services, unemployment, lack of affordable housing, limited public transportation, racism, drug addiction, adolescent pregnancy and waste management. These challenges are found in nearly every community throughout the world to some degree. We can't pick up any local newspaper without seeing an article highlighting these problems. Government services to address these issues are often notoriously inefficient and ineffective.

Over the past 50 years, Non-Government Organizations (NGOs) have been set up to complement government systems. The idea was to use NGOs to balance and boost ongoing public efforts. NGOs were perceived to be less bureaucratic, more flexible and more cost-effective than government approaches. Their procedures proved to be more community-oriented, participatory, client-centered and democratic.

Gradually, NGOs blossomed all over the world with extensive multilateral and bilateral resources being provided to support their efforts. While NGOs have made great strides in helping improve our world, it is also clear that they do not represent the silver bullet that will end the world's woes. For any community to address the myriad problems listed above, government, NGO and general public support are all required.

Interpersonal Relationships

In our interactions with others, we face many challenges. On any given day, we might encounter such emotions as: anger, frustration, jealousy, resentment, arrogance, depression, meanness and sadness. This is part of our human experience. Helping others process these feelings can also be a positive contribution.

Misunderstandings often start with something innocent and then grow into something unintended that triggers unwanted emotional responses. If a person can come to better understand the basic human nature of others, they can be a great help to them. This event, taught me an important lesson about how many simple misunderstandings can lead to interpersonal conflicts.

During one of my many trips to Bangladesh, I was invited to a post-conference reception at a private home. It was a lovely place with plenty of space for the 60 people who attended. I chatted with several of the participants before finding an empty seat on one of the many couches. A small cat jumped onto my lap. I petted it for several minutes and then, without warning, it jumped onto the lap of the woman seated next to me. I thought nothing of it. A friend joined me and we began to talk.

Later that night, Ali, our host, asked, *"Matt, what is it between you and Zareen? She is telling everyone how rude you are."*

Not knowing what he was talking about, I said, *"Who is Zareen?"* He pointed to a woman across the room, the one who had been sitting next to me on the couch. *"I have no idea what you are talking about. I never even spoke to her,"* I replied.

"She said that you picked my cat up and tossed it onto her lap. She called it one of the rudest things she had ever experienced. She hates cats."

I felt baffled until I remembered the cat jumping from my lap onto hers. When I went up to her to explain the simple misunderstanding, she repeatedly said I was a rude man and then stormed off.

Misunderstandings frequently occur. Most happen because of limited information or false assumptions. How many events in our lives are based on the same thing? How many fights and arguments start from a lack of sufficient information?

If we can help others accept that things happen without our knowing all the details, perhaps some of these interpersonal issues could be avoided. Sometimes things "just happen". It is important to give others the benefit of the doubt.

What is the Point?

The world faces many significant issues at all levels – global, national, community and interpersonal. While many of them might seem to have little connection to our daily lives, each of us can play a part in addressing them. For this to happen, we need to understand more about these topics and be open to respond. This can make the difference between a world that suffers and a world that thrives. We all need to focus on what we can practically do to make the world a better place.

Part Two:
Heroes

3

HEROES

The Hero in all of Us

Every issue discussed so far requires a human response and needs us to take action. Whether it's a bold step toward solving a global problem or a simple gesture to help a stranger, each act is part of the collective good.

I consider **everyone who steps up to help, no matter how big or small the gesture, to be a hero**. Each of us has this spirit inside us which needs to be recognized and nurtured to reach its full potential. This is the core message of this book.

Most of us feel that heroes are people who demonstrate impossible feats of bravery to help those in need. While this is one example, not all heroes exist in comic books or in movies. They are not just people who risk their own lives to save the helpless but also ordinary men and women who give of their best selves for others. Why? It is the right thing to do or because they simply can't help themselves.

Most of us have enough generosity of spirit to change the world. Yes, there are bad apples but good will always triumph. We need to develop and foster the good in ourselves and encourage the good in those around us.

Taking this concept further, a heroic act can be something quite simple and seemingly insignificant. A person helps an elderly woman cross a busy intersection; a teacher helps a struggling student with a new concept; a police officer helps the victim of a crime to feel secure after just having been violated; a mother helps her son when he scrapes his knee; a person smiles at another who is having a bad day.

In all of these situations, it is not about the size of the gesture, it is about the affirming gesture itself – **the selfless act of kindness for another without any expectation of something in return**. The gesture can be as subtle as a hand reaching out for another to offer reassurance of love. What is the main ingredient of this act? Doing "something" for another. Why? Because it is the right thing to do.

But let us not forget the rest of the world. These selfless acts go beyond our interactions with other human beings to include what we do for the animals, plants, environment, and the world we live in. Our heroic acts extend to every aspect of our life experience.

Compassion means we care about others, treat them with kindness and feel a strong desire to help people in need. Compassion is a miracle of "empathy combined with action". For a child, this might be expressed by a hug, hand-holding or by saying something kind to help someone who appears to be sad or upset. Children often do this naturally.

But we all have this tendency. If you are walking down the street and the person in front of you trips and falls, you'd help them up. There is no thought involved in this process. It is an automatic response.

Open the windows of one person's compassion and we discover it is contagious. The doors of large efforts toward human improvement often swing on small hinges.

There is a potential hero in all of us. It is a voice of good, of righteous-ness, of action and of love. In this modern world of ours, this voice receives too little nurturing. It lies dormant too much of the time. The possibility of regular, continuous good never reaches its full potential.

This part of ourselves is capable of waking us up to current issues and problems and then encouraging us to help.

For me, a hero is also someone who makes the effort to learn about something and in his or her own way, does something to help. A person doesn't have to completely change their lifestyle to tackle a problem. It could be as simple as educating others, sending money to a struggling charity or volunteering at a local non-profit organization for a few hours a week. Heroism is all about acts of goodness, big or small. They all add up. This is my simple message.

Finally, a hero understands that almost all people respond to goodness, that individuals and individual actions matter, and that regularly showing examples of people being good to each other will inspire similar actions in others.

Recognizing our Heroic Voice

Heroism is that part of our mind that whispers into our thoughts to urge us forward, to step up, to act, to get involved and to do the right thing. There are times when that voice is silent and other times when it is so clear, it is as if someone is shouting at us.

Our inner voice helps us see the path ahead, often persisting until we listen and respond. We can try to ignore it but if we do, we later feel regret. It is the voice of our inherent goodness. We want to help. We want to be involved. We want to have a sense of purpose. When this voice becomes inescapable, we need to surrender.

Confronting a Crisis

The clearest example of the impact of this voice can be found when we are confronted with a crisis. When we come upon a traffic accident, most of us instinctively stop and offer help. Within an instant, we know what needs to be done and we act. We don't have to be taught this – it is part of our core being. Some of us may have had an experience like this one:

> *"I watched as the car in front of me ran off the road and hit the pole. Something told me that I needed to act. I heard the voice in my head. It walked me through what I needed to know. It was as if I was already programmed to act."*

If a person is struggling to hoist their bag into the overhead compartment on a plane, we automatically step forward and help. What needs to be done is so clear, there is no questioning it. In fact, if we chose not to do something, that inner voice becomes louder and louder. Inaction is not an option. For many of us, within our DNA is a genetic response mechanism. This is our inner heroic voice.

Our Motivations

Sometimes those who have suffered in life are more inclined to act heroically than others. People who have been exposed to poverty, oppression and violence understand what it is like to be in need. This experience sensitizes them to those who require help.

When I provided disaster relief as a US government official working for USAID in Sri Lanka immediately after the 2004 tsunami, some of the most dedicated people who stepped forward were those who had experienced the greatest loss. They recalled the pain and despair they had experienced. Some of them mentioned that they got involved in other causes because they felt a need to repay the kindness shown to them. There is something significant about having gone through a tough period that motivates a person to help others through their own pain.

Of the volunteers I have had the honor to work with in the counter-trafficking sector in Hong Kong, at least half seemed to have experienced some major trauma in their life at one time or another. This theme was so prevalent in my work, we once set up a conference to help offer personal healing. Sometimes the motivation is based on a personal recovery; other times the person never really got over the pain they absorbed. But something compels them to help others – as if by doing so, this will lessen their own pain.

Returning a Kindness ✓

During my four-decade career, I have been blessed with great mentors. Much of the benefit I gained from these enlightened people derived from their personal stories. What sometimes surprised me was that while some of those stories initially seemed irrelevant, later in my life they became influential.

One of my most significant mentors told me that he had decided to work with me because he felt he had something to offer. However, he went on to say:

"This is a gift I offer to you. But once you have achieved a similar status in your life, you need to pass this gift on to others. We must all repay kindness. It is not something to be consumed – it is something to be shared and recycled. Promise me you will accept the fact that if we receive, we must also give back."

When I hear my heroic voice, I am often reminded that to give of myself is an honor, a privilege and a responsibility.

The Long Game

Some heroic efforts result from a chance event that requires immediate action – pulling a child out of a burning car, saving a drowning person, or stopping a violent act. These events require a death-defying, split-second response. This is what many of us think of when we define a hero.

There is another form of heroism – the long game, when a person chooses to devote his or her life to the service of others. We see this among service providers who work in health, social work, disaster response, law enforcement, education and human rights. This is heroism in a different form. Unlike the hero who gains the limelight for an instant response, many of these long-term heroic efforts go unsung and unacknowledged. However, they are nonetheless equally valid. The following story is an example:

> *"I have worked in the emergency room for over ten years. Every day we save lives. I sometimes feel that people take our work for granted. What would things be like if we weren't there 24/7? I see people being honored in the papers when they save a kid from something like a car accident. But for us, this happens every day. We don't need to be honored every time this happens. I just wish more people would acknowledge that we do this because we care."*

A Daily Exercise of Goodwill

Our kind deeds have a way of generating more kindness. I would argue that we should all try to take any opportunity to carry out heroic acts on a daily basis. The gratefulness that goes along with these actions can motivate others to follow.

One afternoon, as I was walking down a busy street in Hong Kong, I saw an old woman pushing a cart full of used cardboard. As she crossed the street, her load fell off. Within seconds, people came from all directions to help her. First there was one, then two, then five. Several of these good Samaritans helped to reload the cart. Others directed traffic away from the group. The group worked together as a team to ensure that the load and the woman made it safely to the side of the road.

But this kindness did not end there. One of the bystanders pushed the cart to its final destination. Each of these acts of kindness was small, but combined, they added up to something quite extraordinary. The goodwill that played out enriched each actor in this small drama. The wave of kindness couldn't be stopped. They became a heroic mob.

One of the major questions of our time is: "How do we tap into such generalized goodwill and use it to help save our planet?"

Hopes and Dreams

For some, doing good is an intention that is ever present; it ties in with a person's hopes, dreams and aspirations. Achieving good helps them to fulfill a sense of purpose that aligns with who they are as a person.

> *"I feel I am a good person. I have always felt this way. When I can help, it reinforces this part of myself. I want to be good. I want to be helpful. It is part of my purpose in life. I am so blessed to have this nature."*

If we were to ask the average person how they would like to be remembered, many would say, "I would like to be considered kind, generous and helpful." One comment made by a fifth grader sums this up well:

"I feel good when I help my neighbor. He is old and needs someone to help him do things. It makes me feel so good inside. It feels good to be good."

Offering a Testimony:

The word "testimony" comes from the Greek word *martyria*, which means to offer up "evidence". The root of the word is *martyr*. A loose translation of this word can be stated this way – *the evidence of what nearly killed me.* The term is used to describe a person's journey through hardship or hard times, along with what they did to overcome these challenges. Everyone's testimony is unique.

Anyone who shares a testimony is heroic because they are offering the intimate details of their own personal struggles. This self-exposure may require a person's deepest hurts and fears to be on display. One of my close friends writes:

"There was only one instance where I felt like I was doing something extremely brave, and that involved placing my life under a microscope and writing down the ugliness I experienced in my life so it would help others. When people come up and tell me how much they appreciated my book's honesty, that knowledge thrills my heart."

For those who offer their testimony in this way, it is truly a courageous act. To convey our deepest, darkest hurts to complete strangers makes us vulnerable. We do this with the understanding that we can offer hope and healing to those who are on a similar journey. We often do it out of a conviction that what we learned can benefit those in need. It demonstrates our compassion and encourages others to share and to be vulnerable.

Many people experience trauma and hardship in their lives, resulting from the loss of a loved one, a failed relationship, injustice, physical and emotional abuse, bankruptcy and other hardships. During these very difficult times, we often find ourselves struggling alone. The power of a personal testimony is that it helps us understand that our life experiences don't happen in isolation. At any given moment, many others are going through something similar. When these people find each other, genuine healing can follow. Testimonies offer the means to bring people together because they set the example – *it is OK to share our hurts and feelings.*

Testimonies can also be powerful because people relate to personal stories. It is easy for us to follow the drama that is offered within this form of sharing. In many of my speeches, I tell as many of my own stories as I can. Some of them come in the form of testimonies. One of these testimonies I regularly share reveals my failure to help little Amulya when she really needed me (*please see Chapter 1*). While the moment was deeply painful, many people have described how they live with similar regrets. My confession helps to encourage them to face their own situations because my experience made it real for them.

In some settings, following a testimony, people come together to console each other. I once participated on a panel at a major justice conference. Near the end of this event, the moderator asked the panelists how we dealt with the trauma we often experienced as part of our work. The first speaker cried as he offered his response. Because his work involved rescuing young children from the clutches of pedophiles, he had experienced some heartbreaking things. Through his sobs, he explained how this work had impacted both his personal and professional life in many negative ways.

After he finished, the same question was posed to me. While I have answered this question a hundred times during many events, for some reason, without warning, I found myself bawling like a baby. I could hardly get my words out. I explained that I had seen many horrific things and had learned to hold much of my pain inside but now and then, the door to this part of myself would swing open, often without warning. This was one of those times.

Following this involuntary display of emotion, I felt embarrassed. All I wanted to do was to escape from the auditorium. But as the session was coming to a close, a handful of the participants rushed over to me and thanked me profusely for my honesty. They said that my statements helped them to release some of their own stored-up pain. I learned from this experience how powerful a testimony can be to connect people emotionally and bring them together to help each other.

Finally, testimonies can offer a sense of hope for a resolution. If a person is in the middle of a crisis and can't see a way out, a testimony allows them to understand that others have been faced with similar situations and overcame them.

Falling in Love with our Role as Savior

During one of my trips to China, I took a train from Nanning to Guilin. I love trains and was really excited. I sat by the window, anticipating the wonderful views of the countryside.

In the seat in front of me was a young, loud Australian college student, who spent nearly an hour talking with her friend about how wonderful she was for spending a week volunteering at an orphanage in Cambodia. Nearly everything she said focused on her "*sacrifice*" and her "*immense contribution.*" She said, "*Not too many people would do what I did. I spent a week of my life helping these poor people. They were really lucky to have me there. I could tell I reached them as a role model. I doubt they ever had anyone as good as me."*

As I sat listening to her relentlessly talking about herself in glowing terms, I felt she had completely missed the point. Sometimes volunteers forget the most fundamental objective of their service. It is not about them; it is about the people they serve. This person fell in love with herself as a savior. By doing this work, she felt excessively noble and self-important.

We have all seen examples of this; the person who haughtily states, "*I am working to fight injustice*" in a manner that places the emphasis on themselves. Sometimes a self-satisfied smile goes along with this, as if the person is waiting for recognition or a pat on the back for being so wonderful.

Sadly, I have sometimes acted this way myself. In my younger years, I often lost sight of the victims I was supporting because I was too focused on my own nobility. When I remember that behavior, I feel embarrassed and ashamed. Just thinking about this makes me cringe.

When we work in the service of others, it is important that we put their needs above our own. This life-saving work should not be done for our own self-gratification. We must understand that when we volunteer to help others, we must do a job. We are privileged to serve, not to glorify ourselves. It is about THEM. There is never a downside to being humble.

4

OUR HUMAN EXPERIENCE

What Holds Us Back

Over the years, I have made countless presentations on the topic of human slavery to audiences ranging from 5 to 1,500 at schools, corporations, government entities, churches and libraries. During one year in Hong Kong, I gave 175 talks to nearly 20,000 people.

During this time, I observed four basic tendencies within my audiences.

First, most people seemed to know very little about human slavery. In fact, I'd say less than ten percent of the people knew about even a quarter of what I was talking about. When other global problems are presented in public forums (poverty, global warming, hunger, disparity, etc.), similar levels of awareness can be found. Let's face it: few people have a basic awareness of the major issues of our time. Why is this relevant? Because if you don't know about a problem, you are not going to care about it. And if you don't care, you will do nothing about it. Awareness is essential.

Second, once exposed to such issues, many people immediately begin to care. They are shocked to learn that slavery is so widespread and increasing in today's world, with so many people suffering in these terrible conditions at home and abroad. This reality is extremely disturbing for most of us. Two participants who learned about these issues said:

> *"I am 34 years old and I am finding out about this terrible thing just now? I don't understand why this isn't front page news."*

> *"I feel terrible that the world doesn't do more about this. Now that I know, I want to do something."*

Third, once a person's mind is opened, they begin to consider their options.

> *"Someone needs to step up and help. I wish I knew what to do. Give me something to sign up to."*

> *"I really want to help. I wonder if making a donation to an organization might do. I can't think of anything else."*

And fourth: <u>For most, this stage of feeling a strong desire to take action tends to diminish very quickly</u> – sometimes within 15 minutes after leaving the presentation venue.

> *"I attended that event two weeks ago. When I was there, I was really fired up. But then I got busy. You know how it is; I moved on."*

> *"I signed the volunteer sheet before leaving, but I doubt I'll go. They want to meet on Thursday nights. It's not a good day for me."*

Following many of my presentations, five to ten people often come up to me and say, "I was really touched by what you said. What can I do to help? I'm really serious." While these comments may be sincere at the time, something seems to happen along the way.

Even after handing them my business card and agreeing to work with them, I seldom get more than one or two who follow through. Sometimes none of them do. The momentary intention might be there but the commitment to follow through is sorely lacking.

As I have discussed, modern slavery and many other global issues can't be solved by a few thousand development workers. It can't possibly go away or achieve significant relief until millions of us actively fight evil. We need to understand the great divide between wanting to act and actually acting heroically.

Velleity

Following an emotional presentation I did in Malaysia, my frustration over the lack of public involvement came out in a short rant at the end of my talk. A person from the audience came up to me and said, "*Your talk was all about velleity.*" When my facial expression revealed that I didn't understand what this person was talking about, he went on to define the word for me. "*Velleity means a wish or inclination not strong enough to lead to action*". He said what I described was something the world had faced from the beginning of time. He went on to state that "*people are great at observing and yearning but terrible at following through*".

Crossing the Line

In one of my TEDx talks, I presented another example of velleity. I said: "*Let me explain – there is this line.*" I hold my arm upright. "*On one side of the line, a person learns about an issue, then comes to understand it, then begins to care and then gets right up to this line." I slap my arm to demonstrate that the line has been reached. "The moment we cross this line into action, we are doing something for others or for the world – we are part of the solution. But to get over this line can be one of the most difficult things a person can do. Why is this important? Because this is a line that can change the world. Even the smallest gesture and act can be helpful – an act of kindness or a simple task on behalf of another. It all adds up. But as simple as it is, for many, the journey never reaches its full completion. Why is this so?"*

Our Chronic Fear of Change

Part of the reason for this is our tendency to avoid doing something that may result in change. Even when change is positive, it still involves adjusting to something new. Positive or negative, big or small, change disrupts our daily routine – and can push us out of our comfort zone. Facing change and the unknown can cause fear, worry, dread and uneasiness. Thus, one of the biggest obstacles faced when confronting change is being "paralyzed by the status quo".

Eric Roth, in his screenplay *The Curious Case of Benjamin Button*, sums up this concept nicely:

"For what it's worth: it's never too late or, in my case, too early to be whoever you want to be. There's no time limit; stop whenever you want. You can change or stay the same, there are no rules to this thing. We can make the best or the worst of it. I hope you make the best of it. And I hope you see things that startle you. I hope you feel things you never felt before. I hope you meet people with a different point of view. I hope you live a life you're proud of. If you find that you're not, I hope you have the courage to start all over again."

Roth's statement celebrates the power of change.

Talking Ourselves out of Action

Although it seems simple for us to get involved in causes, few people take up the challenge. To understand why, I interviewed many people who have attended my talks to gain some insight. I found that many of us find ways of talking ourselves out of taking action. Below are some of the arguments we use.

I'm too Busy

One of the most prevalent reasons for not getting involved is, *"I'm too busy. I can't fit anything more into my life."*

What are we busy doing? According to international media surveys, the world's average television consumption ranges from 154 to 292 minutes per day. This means that many people spend more than two hours a day watching television.

Other studies show the average person spends up to four hours a day on their telephones and other devices. Most modern people are spending a full quarter of their waking hours staring at a screen. The five top social media platforms eating into our time, include Facebook, Instagram, Twitter, Snapchat and YouTube.

Several hours of TV watching and iPhone gazing could be better dedicated to doing something more useful and related to a cause. Thus, the *"I'm too busy"* argument isn't valid for many of us. For the most part, we choose what we want to do.

These Things are too Far Away

For some, a global issue like trafficking seems important but it is a problem that is far away – something happening in countries like

Nepal, Thailand or China. It is placed into a category of *"things that are upsetting but remote"*. Despite explaining to audiences that the issue is widespread and happening in their own country and community, it doesn't seem to register. This is often apparent in comments made at the end of my presentations:

> *"What can I do to help? What you are describing happens in developing countries. It is so far away. There is nothing I can do."*
>
> *"I feel sorry for those poor people. But if the oceans rise and Bangladesh is covered with water, that is halfway around the world."*
>
> *"What happens in Africa should be left to the Africans. It is not our problem."*

Human trafficking happens in every developed country and its effects actually impact us all. It is estimated that Atlanta, Georgia, has up to 200 new sex trafficking victims every month. If we choose to buy a £2.50 T-shirt in a London discount store, we could be supporting a sweatshop in Vietnam that exploits people. The relevance of this issue is not far away. It is right in our own backyard.

Likewise, many community issues happen in our familiar neighborhoods. Instead of saving the world, we can save our small corner of the world. Many local efforts address concerns such as: homelessness, unemployment, drug abuse, litter and loneliness. There is no need to look far away; the problems in this world often land on our doorstep. A town official I once met said this about his community:

"Everyone is a critic. They complain about the things we do. They complain about the things we don't do. They never seem satisfied with anything. I wish these people could see the world through my eyes. There are so many complicated problems. It is never easy. If they don't like something going on in our town, they can do something about it. I'm so tired of their bitching and moaning. I wish I could tell some of these people to just step up or shut up."

What if I Don't Like it?

Some people don't volunteer because they fear that once they get involved, they won't like the experience. *"It would be awkward if I decided to walk away. Better not to get involved in the first place."*

Let's face it, much of our life experience is based on trial and error. If we try something and like it, we continue. If not, we leave. Most NGOs would prefer that a person tries something then walks away if it isn't right for them than to have people never make the attempt. One NGO director put it this way:

"Humanitarian work is not for everyone – you either like it or you don't. Most people don't know what they want to do until they step into our shoes. I'd rather every person who might want to make an effort step up. If many of them walk away – then OK. Whatever. At least they know. But usually some take to it and continue. Most won't know which group they fall into until they experience our world. So, I say open yourself up and just try. You have nothing at all to lose."

I'll Get Around to It Someday

Many of the people I spoke to said that they planned to get involved, but they just haven't got around to it yet. Volunteering is something that many people have decided they will do but not tomorrow, or next week, or next month or even next year. It will happen sometime in the undetermined future.

> *"Every year I put 'saving the world' on my to-do list. I just never get around to doing it. But there is always next year."*
>
> *"I will write out my New Year's resolutions in two months. I will include something on this list then. I always do."*

Many who say such things appear very serious about wanting to get involved. They just can't do it anytime soon. They often propose a time that follows a milestone that must be reached. It's convenient to visualize all you will do for people after:

- You retire
- You graduate
- You get married
- Your child grows up
- Your work schedule settles down
- Your next promotion

People who make this comment appear to feel OK about their inaction because they have decided to get involved eventually – just not now. The disconnect comes when the intended action never happens. When this is pointed out to them, many are surprised. They defend their stance with conviction:

"I said I'll do something and I will. I need some more time. You'll see."

"That isn't fair. Things keep coming up. I plan to help. I said I would."

Every Life Matters

A recurrent issue I face when making presentations is the fatalistic view that human slavery problems are too overwhelming and pervasive to tackle. The disparity between 40 million victims and only 100,000 people rescued causes people to question me. They ask, "With so many victims, it seems impossible to make a difference. Why should we even try?" The question arises again and again. One person said:

> *"I feel that the problem is too large and my contribution would only be a drop in a huge bucket. I feel paralyzed at times if I feel I'm not getting to the root cause of the problem."*

Many people feel that their contribution to a big problem would be small, so why bother doing anything?

I respond to these people with the well-known Starfish Story, a simple parable that makes the important point:

> *"A father and son walk along a beach covered with stranded starfish. Every few feet, the father stoops to pick up a starfish and toss it back into the ocean. At some point, the son looks*

at the immense stretch of sand, full of dying starfish, and says, 'Father, there is no way you can save all of these starfish. What difference does it make?' The wise father pauses to toss another starfish to safety. In a gentle voice he responds, 'It made all the difference to that one.' In other words, every life is important - every life matters."

Like other global issues, the human slavery problem feels so big and so unmanageable that it can easily shut us down emotionally. But this mustn't stop us from doing whatever we can with what we have. To each person rescued, it makes a VERY big difference. The world gains back a precious grain of humanity with every victim saved from a terrible life.

We are always talking about making a difference in this world, yet we think that we ourselves can't make a difference because we are only one person. If we think that there is something wrong with the world we live in, we need to change it. We need to take action.

How does this relate to the hero within you? When we work on this or any other cause, victory comes one life or one achievement at a time. Eventually, the numbers will add up to something we never thought possible.

"I used to think that my efforts couldn't possibly matter. But then I realized that if everyone said this, nothing would be done. So now I do my share and hope others will do the same. A tiny speck of sand can be part of a beach. What makes a beach special are the many specks of sand. It is the same idea. Small becomes large when everyone gets involved. During a recent hike, I began to pick up discarded water bottles. I

managed to collect about 20 along the way. OK, so there are another 1 trillion more out there in our oceans and forests. But I can say there are now 20 less."

It is too Sad

Some people find it hard to face some of the sad and depressing issues of our time. After a talk I gave in Canada, one woman said:

"I didn't like your talk. It made me feel sad and depressed. I wish I hadn't come. The information you shared completely ruined my day. I don't want to feel this way."

This desire to avoid being exposed to contentious issues comes up all the time in my work:

"When I think about all of the many problems faced by the world, it makes me cringe. I really don't like to face them."

"Whenever I see those kids on the TV in those poor countries, I change the channel. It breaks my heart to witness their suffering."

To avoid these feelings, some people will simply ignore the topic altogether. I know this because of the reactions people reported about my book on forced prostitution – *Captive Daughters*. This novel goes into great detail about the horrors of sex trafficking. Many people who start to read it don't get past page 36, where a graphic rape scene unfolds. Why? They get to this section and the content puts them off. They say things like, "*It is too sad. It depresses me. I don't want to expose myself to something like this.*"

Here you have a person who is sitting in his or her living room on their couch, with the air conditioning on, a cup of coffee in their hand and they can't even face words on a page. Imagine if one of us were on the receiving end of this brutality? Shouldn't such a terrible reality spur us to act?

I agree that the topic of human slavery is a hard one. It displays much of the worst life has to offer: rape, torture, abuse, pain, suffering, depression, oppression, despair and early death. There really is no way to sugarcoat it. The same can be said of all other global issues. Poverty, hunger, disease and disparity are all cruel, difficult topics to confront. For us to combat these problems, we must understand, feel the pain and act. We must be spurred into action despite our squeamishness. We must learn the horrific facts, then get involved. More than 40 million slaves around the world cry out: "*Where are you?*" We must provide an answer.

Looking back over the years, I realize that those of us working in the anti-slavery world have contributed to the problem. We hit people over the head repeatedly with information and messages that are too graphic. This immediately puts them off. A closed mind is incapable of offering any help to those suffering. This is a missed opportunity. We need to offer a more subtle approach so people are not overwhelmed.

We need to strike a balance between informing people about the horrors of injustice while at the same time suggesting things they can do to make a difference.

From a fundraiser's perspective, it's important to note that when we tell a sad story that has a happy ending and show people how they can be involved in creating more happy endings, they are more likely to be supportive. People want to be part of something that is successful.

In Bangladesh, I would see the most beautiful lotus flowers growing in a disgusting cesspool. In even the most terrible situations, we can find promise for beauty, love, hope and the possibility of positive change. Had I not believed this, I could not have worked among human cesspools in beautiful countries for more than 35 years.

Be the Change

I often hear people say, *"I'm just a student or a housewife or a government worker – what do I have to offer?"* This is one of the most frustrating statements I hear. As human beings, we all have something to offer. It isn't a matter of our age or experience, it is a matter of our willingness to step up.

During my time at the United Nations, a nine-year-old girl contacted me and said, *"Mr Friedman, I saw you in a documentary and I want to volunteer."* I said to her, *"You are only nine years old."* Her response was, "so what?" I repeated my statement and she said, *"so what"* again. I asked her what she felt she could offer. Her response was, *"I'm good at finding things on the Internet."* So, I gave her a chance. As it turned out, this young girl excelled at finding information related to human trafficking cases. In fact, I'd go as far as saying that she was better than my second-year Yale law students at locating data. She had an inherent gift in this area.

What is my point? We all have God-given gifts. Some of us are gifted at singing, dancing, public speaking, writing, planning, creating strategies, raising money or even selling T-shirts. It is important to find a way to identify our gifts and use them. Examples of this in my own work to raise awareness of human trafficking include:

- A banking professional helped write a typology report that broke criminal behavior into component parts.
- A nine-year-old American girl raised $15,000 selling lemonade to help victims of human slavery.

- A college student regularly went to retail stores and politely asked the managers how they ensured the products they sold were slave-free. Eventually, they all offered positive answers. Their main offices took note.
- A church leader set up a sweatshop challenge, asking participants to repeatedly screw nuts onto bolts then immediately unscrew them from 8pm until 6am (ten consecutive hours) without food, water or sleep. The event helped participants experience what slaves often endure.
- A housewife wrote letters to newspapers, magazines and television stations to encourage them to publicize human trafficking and slavery issues. They did.
- A churchgoer set up a "Battle of the Bands" song-writing contest to create awareness among music lovers. Musicians accepted the challenge and wrote ten amazing songs.
- A mother of three convinced her library to stock books on this subject.
- A college student set up a film festival that reached 5,000 students.
- A father of three persuaded the motels in his city to place the local anti-trafficking hotline number in every office and every room.
- A student group sent letters to their state lawmakers asking them to focus on this issue.
- A fifth-grader encouraged his local school board to partner with students to include the issue of modern-day slavery in their curriculum.

Each person used their personal strengths and experiences to make something happen. Mahatma Gandhi summed up this concept well with his famous quote: *"Be the change that you wish to see in the world."*

What do I Really Want to Do?

Some people can't move forward because they don't know what they want to do. I hear people say things like this all the time:

> *"I still don't know what my cause is. I have tried watching and reading everything I can get my hands on. I care about so many things. With so many choices, I don't know where to begin."*

> *"I care about the world. I really do. But there are so many places I want to help. There are too many options."*

Several years ago, I had a series of meetings with a Hong Kong-based billionaire who decided he wanted to donate some of his fortune to address social issues. While I urged this person to invest in efforts to combat human trafficking, he wasn't sure if this was the right thing for him to do. He kept saying, *"There are so many other things I can support."* To help him make a decision, I suggested that he meet with people who supported other causes. Three years later he still couldn't decide which cause to support. Sometimes having too many options can be an obstacle. People don't know where to start so they do nothing at all.

I'm Fine

One of our biggest stumbling blocks to motivating ourselves to engage is a feeling of contentment. On the surface, most of us would say that feeling content is something to strive for. If a person is truly content, without regrets, desires or aspirations, it results in a feeling of well-being and ease. This is a good thing but it also acts as an avoidance technique because it reduces our motivation to explore life and to make changes:

> *"When I was young, I felt restless about things. Nowadays, that feeling seems to be missing. My motivation engine is just not fueled. I don't feel the need any more."*

Contentment can be like thirst. Most of the time you drink enough without thinking about it. At other times, we feel really thirsty and that motivates us to drink more.

Some of the most effective leaders of our time have understood this fact. Mahatma Gandhi once said: *"Healthy discontent is the prelude to progress."* There is power in discontentment just as there is power in thirst.

The Great Debate

Sometimes we are confronted with a situation where we have the choice to act or to walk away. While our heroic voice might drive us to act, a counter voice tells us to walk away – to leave it to someone else. In these circumstances, if we are by ourselves, we often don't have much choice.

However, if there are others around, our mind argues: *"There are other people here. Let one of them get involved, not me."* Or in some cases, you might think, *"If no one else is stepping up, why should I?"* The voice tells us to step down, to hold back, to stay put. It lulls us into complacency. Research tells us that the more people witnessing an incident, the less likely any of them will get involved. This is known as, *the bystander effect.*

This is our daily mental challenge: the heroic voice versus our "I'm content" voice – the whiny, doubtful, fearful one. The solution is to stop the discussion and simply surrender. Take the leap of faith and see where it leads.

> *"Part of me felt like running for my life. Then I heard a voice in my head saying that I needed to act. I couldn't stop myself. The voice was right. I had to do something, so I did."*

A true hero ignores this mind chatter and says to himself, "*I don't care if no one is helping, I'm going to do it anyway.*"

What has this got to do with me?

For a long time, many people talked about global warming and the need to do something about it. But this message didn't spread. Then, in 2008, Al Gore's film, *An Inconvenient Truth*, was released. The first reaction nearly everyone had after seeing this film? "*It was a wake-up call.*" *An Inconvenient Truth* helped moviegoers realize that their actions had an impact. They could be part of the solution, rather than just contributing to the problem.

Gore made the issue relevant to our lives by concluding:

> *"Each one of us is a cause of global warming, but each one of us can make choices to change that with the things we buy, the electricity we use, the cars we drive; we can make choices to bring our individual carbon emissions to zero. The solutions are in our hands, we just have to have the*

determination to make it happen. We have everything that we need to reduce carbon emissions, everything but political will. But in America, the will to act is a renewable resource."

Despite what most people think, human slavery has relevance to our life in many ways. First, as citizens in this world, every human rights abuse is relevant to us all. Slavery represents a major human rights violation. We, as human beings, must care about the people we share this world with. As rights bearers ourselves, we must all accept some responsibility. Thus, if women and children are forced into prostitution, society must accept responsibility and help to address the problem. Up until now, this responsibility has been embraced by very few.

Second, as consumers we all contribute to human slavery. Data shows 75 percent of the trafficking cases are forced labor cases and 60 percent of these cases are associated with supply chains. Supply chains are the companies and sources of materials involved in the production of the items we buy. With so many businesses in our supply chains utilizing forced labor, we have all purchased goods that are directly or indirectly associated with slavery, and congratulated ourselves on finding bargains. It is a reality we cannot ignore.

Understanding that we can alter our purchasing behaviors to reduce slavery allows us to accept responsibility for being a part of the problem and our responsibility to reduce it.

The same arguments can be made for most global issues. We just need to be open to this idea.

NGO Transparency and Trust

Another reason why some people don't get involved is that they believe that charities and NGOs efforts are somehow unethical. Over the years, there have been many stories and articles about scandals related to program outcomes, a lack of transparency and misuse of funding.

> "I keep reading stories about the NGO world. Some of them are really not that honest. They collect money and don't use it. I don't know if I want to be a part of something like this."

> "The newspapers are filled with articles that demonstrate that civil society is not all that good."

There are many reasons for this trend. First, there is a feeling that many charities are not transparent. People want to know what an organization is doing before they get involved to help. If this information isn't available, there is suspicion that perhaps something is being hidden.

> "I went online and couldn't figure out what most of the organizations dealing with animal rights were doing. I want to know what I'm getting involved in before I offer my time."

> "I heard that many charities use most of the money to cover fundraising. That doesn't seem right to me."

Some people feel that volunteering for an NGO will result in drudgery. There appear to be many stories out there that talk about how interns only fetch coffee and carry out menial administrative tasks:

> "I have heard how NGOs have volunteers do slave labor. If I am going to give my time, I want to feel that my contribution really has some value."

We also hear of examples of people who have been seriously burned from an NGO experience.

"I stepped up to a big thing once and got sued, and then realized I had been duped to get into it in the first place. Be sure you are not just being manipulated."

There are enough of these stories out there for people to feel cynical and cautious about the world of charity. This kind of information helps to feed the voice in our mind that talks us out of doing things. One way to overcome this concern is to spend more time researching which organizations meet a higher standard. It is also important to get referrals from others who have worked with a particular group. Doing this due diligence can help to overcome this concern. Finally, there are also charity watchdog organizations like Charity Watch and Charity Navigator that offer insights about nonprofit organizations.

The Heart of the Matter

Brain research tells us that we are more likely to respond to advertisements that show us one hungry child rather than many. Part of the reason for this boils down to empathy. When an issue can be focused on a child's face or a single abandoned animal, their individual plight moves us and motivates us to act. We can easily relate to a problem of this size.

This is part of the reason the human trafficking sector hasn't been successful when we talk about the massive number of modern slaves – 40 million. When we hear about this many people in dire need, we tend to tune it out. While our mind can intellectually grasp the magnitude of this issue, our brain has a hard time getting our head around this amount of suffering or pain. Thus, the issue becomes an abstraction that seems beyond our control.

I learned this fact many years ago. When I start any of my talks, I begin with a story about a single individual. I offer details about her life both before and after she was abducted. I give this person a face, a name and an identity. I make her real to the audience. This allows people to relate to the victim and have a better understanding of the human cost. Doing this keeps me from assuming that if they feel the problem is massive, they will help out of a sense of responsibility. As we have learned, the opposite is actually closer to the truth.

I Don't Know How to Begin

Some are ready to volunteer, get involved and commit their time but they just don't know where to start. Having little access to any information about the NGO world, they don't have a clue how to take that first step. Every person who reaches this point but then loses interest because the path forward is unclear is a missed opportunity.

> *"I was ready. I decided to do my part. But I couldn't figure out how to do this. There was no one to take me through this process. After a while, the feeling faded."*

All or Nothing Attitude

Another reason that people don't get involved is this idea that to do so would require a great sacrifice or a major life-altering contribution. This feeling is summed up well in these two comments:

> *"How can I do this kind of work? Where is the time? I can't keep up with everything going on in my life. There isn't any room for one more thing."*

"Until hearing this talk, I guess I always thought that if I did my part, I'd have to do something big and time consuming. It always felt like an all or nothing prospect."

I often counter the statement with a question: *"Do you think it would be possible to carve out one hour in a month to help the world? Would this amount of commitment sound like too much?"* Nearly everyone I ask this question agrees, *"Yes, I could do that."* Some add: *"But I thought much more would be needed."* Not understanding how much is being asked can prevent people from doing anything at all.

Heroic activities do not necessarily require us to radically change our lives. It never has to be all or nothing. There is so much in between. If a person feels the commitment is beyond their ability, they simply need to lower their expectations.

When we turn off lights to reduce electricity, when we pick up trash and throw it away, when we offer a helping gesture and when we donate to a worthy cause, we are being heroic. These actions can become habits. The more we integrate them into our life, the less they feel extraordinary.

Other Distractions

For some, life is filled with a constant stream of information and data that is fed to them through their phones, tablets and computers. Because of the immense amount of information, my presentation just adds to their "stream of consciousness". Since there is so much of this "data noise", stopping to take note of one topic would slow the process. They'd fall behind.

For some, complacency, apathy and a sense of indifference prevails in everything. Their lives close in around themselves, built upon a selfish understanding of *"what I can do for me"*. This spirit is often nurtured by the sentiment that life should be all about happiness, prosperity and fun. Nothing else really matters. There is little room in this equation for helping others.

Finally, for some, the idea of doing something is so foreign and so against the grain that it is simply not possible. They wouldn't know what to do. Their life is dominated by complacency, apathy and an overriding feeling that it is not their problem.

Mining Goodwill and Hope

Now and then I ask my audiences to raise their hand if they feel compelled to do their part after hearing one of my talks. Without hesitation, nearly every hand goes up. I can see the desire in their faces, in the way they stretch their hands out. It is a tangible force for good.

While there is no shortage of goodwill within the general public, it is not something that is easy to tap into. For the world to benefit from these feelings, understanding how to "mine" this human factor is one of the major challenges of our time. When I look out at these audiences, I often wonder: "*How do we take this goodwill and use it? How do we sustain these feelings? How do we help these people to understand that within each of us is the potential to be counted?*"

The difference between what our world is and what our world could be depends on humanity's response. We all have choices. We can choose to see, feel and react to needs like these or we can choose to close our eyes and shut our ears.

For the past three years, I have been passionate about understanding how this process works. My simple question is this: "*What can be done to help people go from having basic information about important social issues, to understanding it and then caring enough to actually make personal and significant contributions?*"

How do we help people counter the negative influences against their own heroic desires? How can we replace indifference and indecision with decisive action?

After years of presenting, I know what to say to open the hearts of most people but I still struggle with what I need to do to inspire real change.

As Edmund Burke once wrote: "*The only thing necessary for the triumph of evil is for good men to do nothing.*"

5

WHAT IS OUR PURPOSE?

Defining our Purpose

One of the age-old questions that many of us grapple with in our lives is, "*What is my ultimate purpose?*" There are many possible criteria used for determining our personal answer. Below are a few typical responses:

- *My purpose is to find happiness*
- *My purpose is to make money and live a good life*
- *My purpose is to live a life that matters to others – to serve*
- *My purpose is to honor my spouse and raise my kids well*
- *My purpose is to be the best person I can be*
- *My purpose is to become the CEO*
- *My purpose is to serve God*

Most of these answers respond to an overall outcome. In other words, if my life was to be evaluated, I would have achieved this goal.

These goals are reevaluated at different times in our lives. What we say when we are 20, 30, 40 or 80 often changes. When I was 25, I would say my purpose was "*to live a good life*". After experiencing many things in Nepal, I realized that I wanted more than that – I wanted to serve others. These two statements sum up this conclusion:

> *"Over the years, I have seen my values change from serving myself to serving others."*

> *"My purpose in life can't be summed up with a single statement. It has been a rollercoaster ride for me. Ask me again in two months and I'll give you a different answer."*

In different parts of South Asia, I met businessmen who were ruthless in their corporate dealings. However, when they reached a point of retirement, many of them began to donate large portions of their fortunes to religious institutions or community projects. One of these people sums this process up succinctly:

> *"When I ran the business, I realized that I was consumed with making money. Now that I'm retired and I look back on things, I can see that I was very selfish and full of greed. It is time for me to make up for this. It is never too late."*

A Season for Everything

Throughout my career, I have met many people of all ages who have expressed a feeling of emptiness or an absence of purpose. They might have lives that offer many advantages – employment, advancement and security but something is missing.

> *"I feel like I should be more happy. I seem to have everything I need. But I continue to feel like something is missing. I don't know what it is."*

> *"There is a hole in my life. I can't make out what my purpose is. There has to be something more. I keep looking for it."*

"I don't think I ever stopped to ask what my purpose was. I can't really answer this. I have no idea. I think most people feel the same way. It is a good question."

During my last year working for the United Nations in Bangkok, 2012, I began traveling to Hong Kong to talk to business leaders about modern slavery. With 75 percent of trafficking victims associated with the private sector, my team and I wanted to hear what business leaders had to say about this problem.

Many of these meetings had similar dynamics. When my project assistant set up a meeting three months in advance, they accepted. The UN had a way of opening doors but now and then when I arrived at the office, the reaction that I received changed. Several of these people appeared distressed that they had accepted this meeting. I even overheard one of them remark, *"I forgot all about this. I don't know why I accepted. Oh well, I might as well get it over with."*

In this case, the person I was talking to declared he only had 15 minutes to meet with me. He said he had *"real work to do"*, typing emails into his iPhone while I talked but within five minutes, there was a change in him. Like most of my presentations, my introduction included a dark story related to human trafficking. As I continued, his eyes turned away from his screen and focused on me. In time, he put the phone down and I had his full attention. Despite his initial statement about his availability, the conversation lasted for nearly 90 minutes.

This was not an isolated incident – it seemed to happen all the time. During these talks, a few patterns emerged. First, it appeared that the person was being exposed to this serious issue for the first time. Their mind was suddenly open to hearing more. Second, once they came to understand the extent of the trafficking problem and its relevance to their business, they began to ask more questions. From their facial expressions, they were shocked and even a bit overwhelmed by the topic. What I learned from this was that most people don't know much about what is happening in this most sinister part of the world. When a meeting like this takes place, participants are forced to face the dark reality and it captures their attention.

Yet the story doesn't end here. Within the 30 or so meetings I had in Hong Kong, I couldn't help but feel that many of the people I interviewed seemed sad or a bit depressed. I couldn't understand why. Many of them were at the top of their game, having power, prestige, money and security. As a person who has done service work for much of my life, it appeared that they had things that I once longed to acquire. I couldn't understand why they weren't beaming with happiness. Finally, I asked them why they felt this way. To my surprise, many gave the same answer:

> *"I don't know what it is. I just feel that my life lacks purpose."*
>
> *"Sometimes I feel empty inside. I seem to have everything I need. But there still seems to be something missing. I can't put my finger on it."*
>
> *"I realize there is something more out there. I don't know what it is."*

Finding Balance in Life

What I came to realize was how many people are out of balance. As many high achievers eventually discover, they take from life. They take power, prestige and material wealth but it isn't their fault. Currently, the world's system rewards ambition and success.

However, few of them give anything back. I don't mean reaching into their pocket to make a donation. I mean giving of themselves – helping to serve the world in some way.

When our lives are so out of kilter, we feel it. Our heart and soul longs for meaning. I would go as far as to say that taking and giving need to be in balance for us to feel genuine happiness. If you question this, simply ask your family and friends if they feel there is a good balance between what we receive in life and what we offer. Most of us would admit we should do more.

I find that as we get older, this desire to give back becomes stronger. As young people, we often are self-centered by nature. We focus on making our mark. We want to find our way. But as soon as we become settled and life offers stability, our desires often change.

Transformation

Helping others can be a great way to fill this void. Many people tell me how their involvement in some type of cause defines their purpose. There is an inherent joy that goes along with having a positive impact on this world.

When I was organizing The Mekong Club, which aims to unite and mobilize the private sector to end modern slavery, I asked some of the businesspeople I interviewed to volunteer or join our board. Among those who accepted, I observed an immediate change. As the balance in their lives shifted, they became happier and more fulfilled. Their testimonials are gratifying:

> *"I really feel good about myself. I now realize I can do my job and also help the world. That void is gone."*
>
> *"My kids think it is so cool that I am helping to end modern slavery. I don't know why it took me so long to do this. I wish I had started earlier."*

"I didn't understand the balance thing until it was explained. Now it makes sense to me. There are probably many factors in our daily lives that are out of balance. We need to spend more time focusing on sorting this out."

The Death of Ivan Ilych

When I was 16 years old, I read Tolstoy's short story, *The Death of Ivan Ilych*. Ivan Ilych grew up in Russia. Like most young men of means, he went to the right school, married the right woman, got the right job and moved up in the system. But along the way, he lost track of his life and followed a path that took him far from his initial idealistic hopes and dreams. Following an accident that resulted in a chronic injury, he had several weeks to look back on his life. During this process, he came to the sober realization that he had lived his life all wrong. But with death nearly upon him, there was nothing he could do to change this reality.

This story had a major impact on my life. I remember thinking that I had seen people like Ivan who had reached a particular point in their life when they suddenly woke up, reflected on their present situation and realized they were not happy. In some cases, this scenario evolves into what is often called a *"midlife crisis"*.

The reason behind each ideological crisis differs from person to person. Some severely regret not achieving goals in their life related to work, personal growth, artistic and creative accomplishments, or supporting their children. Others come to feel they have never given much of themselves in support of others. The good news is, it's never too late to get involved. At this critical point, most need someone to guide them through the process. Without this helping hand, many will feel regret, accept this feeling as inevitable and fail to change their lives.

At the end of life there should be few regrets and, in particular, we should feel that our life has had meaning and purpose. Therefore, we should help anyone who wants to contribute to find their particular niche. It is also important that you regularly take stock of your life and ask the questions, *"Am I happy, am I doing what I want, am I living my life the way I want?"* If not, change it.

Young People

While I implied that transformation generally happens later in life, I would like to qualify this statement. Each year I make presentations to students all over the world. I find that many of them worry about the world and want to help. In fact, some students have had this spirit from the time they were very young.

At nearly every school event, one or two students will come up to me and say they want to eventually do my kind of work. Some go on to say that their dream is to work for the United Nations. Over the years, some of these students fulfilled that ambition. One girl I met who was in the seventh grade went on to get a degree in international development, then went to work for the same United Nations' project I had managed.

Many young people have a clear understanding of right and wrong. When they see an injustice, they feel compelled to speak out about it. The problem is that, unfortunately, many of them lack the confidence. They question whether they have anything to offer. As I said earlier, there are many arguments against an innate desire to act and feelings telling us that we cannot do an effective job.

One of the major challenges of our time is to find ways to work successfully with students of all ages. If youthful energy and vitality could be effectively channelled, this would create a force for good that could change the world. In the following chapters, I will discuss this topic in more detail.

Alignment of the Stars

Throughout our life, we go through many stages. Each one is based on a set of circumstances that outline our priorities at that time. Certain milestones are relevant to this process, including a new job, marriage, having children, a promotion or a move to another city. Each of these changes requires time and energy to adjust.

In between these milestones, some of us come to the realization that we want a change. If this change has something to do with offering support for a cause, our minds and hearts are open to an opportunity. Depending on our circumstances, these opportunities come and go. If the right combination of factors is in place, a person might well decide to join a cause, volunteer and get involved.

6

SUPERHEROES

Over the years, movies about superheroes have dominated the box office and become some of the most successful films in recent times. The success of these franchises is rooted in human nature. Deep down, we all want to be reminded of the potential good that prevails in humanity and superheroes inevitably display this spirit. With so much bad news, we need something to offer us a sense of hope. Through these films, we see how someone is able to take charge and uphold good. There are a number of reasons for this phenomenon.

Escapism – Going beyond our own Life Experience

Some people appreciate this superhero genre because it offers a form of escapism. We reflect upon our own ordinary, mundane lives and realize that deep down we yearn for something more meaningful and heroic. We live vicariously through the characters that unfold on screen.

> *"I wish I could be a superhero. In the movies, these characters live such exciting lives. I wish I could help people like that. I sometimes fantasize about this."*

"Superheroes are so awesome. They take evil and give it a black eye. They know how to save lives."

It is no accident that some of the most popular shows on TV include those that focus on the police, lawyers, medical care and emergency response. These shows offer another kind of escapism.

The Embodiment of all that is Good

At their best, superheroes embody good and act as a beacon of light. Against all odds, they take up a cause that reflects the values many of us hold dear – justice, righteousness, optimism and a sense of hope. Their actions set an example for what many of us feel is missing today – sincere, courageous leaders who will fight for us at any cost. Anyone who plays this kind of role is admired and respected. Deep down, many of us long to have these same qualities. In a world where negativity often abounds, their goodness represents a breath of fresh air. By watching these superhero films, we can dream of a better world.

"I wish I could be a superhero. I'd go after all those bad guys and set the world right."

"Superheroes are so brave and good. They don't care about themselves. They care about all of us. I so admire what they do in films. If only it was real."

We Want to be Special

Each of us wants to feel special, recognized and honored in some way. In these films, characters who have these powers are often honored, at least by the end of the movie. Many of us are drawn to these stories because they demonstrate how a person's life can be significant, even if it is fiction.

I once made a presentation to fifth graders. At the end of the talk, I asked the students how many of them wanted to be superheroes. Nearly all of them raised their hands.

> *"If I was a superhero, my power would be to fly. I'd go from place to place and help find the bad people. Everyone will love me."*
>
> *"If I was a superhero, all of my friends would like me more. They'd think that I was someone special. This would make me feel good inside."*

Longing to be admired and respected appears to be in our DNA. This recognition is universally sought. When we see a story play out on a screen with this outcome, we yearn to have a similar experience. This is why the home run that wins the game is dramatized in so many movie themes. Having a huge crowd stand up and clap for the underdog who overcame amazing obstacles to bring about a victory is so appealing and satisfying. We harbor a hidden desire to be this person in our own life. We watch these movies to vicariously experience such heroism.

Superheroes are Just Like Us

Superheroes have no shortage of traumatic experiences. Most superheroes are portrayed as being average people – having both strengths and weaknesses like all of us. Many characters also have back-stories that reveal the hardships and vulnerabilities they had to endure. For example, Peter Parker in Spiderman is just an ordinary guy struggling with his hopes and dreams.

Sometimes our own feelings of disempowerment draw us to these action figures. Despite their difficulties, they offer us hope through the strength of their character and the morality they display. This spirit allows them to overcome evil to bring about good in this world. We all admire this struggle:

> *"Many of the superheroes seem like regular people most of the time. Then something happens and they jump into action. I wonder if there are people out there like that in real life."*

> *"If those superheroes can overcome their problems and still manage to save the world, maybe there is hope for me."*

Good Overcomes Evil

We also watch these movies because we want to see good triumph over evil. We long to see hope in our world restored. We feel comfort in knowing that there is someone who is willing to fight against all odds for justice.

In a blog post about our obsession with superheroes, blogger, Andrew Berryhill once wrote:

> *"In a fallen world full of evil and misfortune, people cling to superheroes as symbols of virtue that conquer both villains and their own weaknesses, giving a glimmer of hope in a frequently dark world".*

People can look to superheroes as beacons of selflessness in an age often perceived as corrupt and full of negativity. Despite their rough and broken outward appearance, many of them carry the culture of charity and sacrifice into the darkest and most savage parts of this world. They guard the weak, the poor and the innocent.

In the counter-trafficking world, I have met many real-life superheroes, who take on the vilest crimes and do whatever they can to stop them from happening. I have seen them among police officers, social workers, lawyers, doctors and even regular citizens of any age. We don't have to look to the movies to find them. They are out there. They are the unsung heroes who do this work every day.

If I had Superpowers?

During many of my presentations, I ask members of the audience to reveal what they would do with superpowers. I am often surprised with the answers. First, I have never had a person say they would use these powers to do something negative. The most typical answer focuses on doing good:

> *"I would fly around and use my powers to save people from the hands of criminals."*
>
> *"If I had superpowers, I'd go to places that had disasters and use my powers to save people. It would feel so good to be this kind of hero."*
>
> *"I'd show that good always wins over evil."*

The fact that good is such a priority is a positive outcome. If we could only help people to understand that they already have superpowers – the ability to help solve the world's problems – we'd have far fewer troubles.

Superhero Quotes

The people who write comic books and screenplays also understand the power of superheroes. In many of the scripts, you find motivational quotes that are meant to inspire us all, and they do:

"It's not who I am underneath but what I do that defines me."

Batman

"Heroes are made by the path they choose, not the powers they are graced with."

Iron Man

"With great power comes great responsibility."

Spiderman

"What happens when the unstoppable force meets the immovable object? They surrender."

Superman

"I believe there's a hero in all of us, that keeps us honest, gives us strength, makes us noble, and finally allows us to die with pride, even though sometimes we have to be steady, and give up the thing we want the most. Even our dreams."

Spiderman

"A true hero isn't measured by the size of his strength, but by the size of his heart."

Zeus

"Life doesn't give us purpose. We give life purpose."

The Flash

These statements are inspiring. They encourage us to think about our own lives and ask the question, "*Can I, too, hold myself to a higher standard? Can I follow a similar noble course?*" I know this because I feel the same way when I hear these quotes. I want to improve myself, I want to be a better person and I want to reach a higher standard.

Real Life Superheroes

Real life superheroes are the ones who protect our streets, guard our freedom, put out our fires, save us after accidents take place, offer care to us when we are ill and counsel us when we are in need. Our world is filled with these caregivers and service providers who dedicate their lives to help others. Sometimes we don't appreciate their immense sacrifice until we are faced with a crisis ourselves.

We must also include the people who teach us. Teachers take our evolving minds and hearts and shape them – helping us reach our full potential. Teachers have significantly changed me in good ways. They were there to meet the exact need I had at that time. We are fortunate if we have such examples in our lives. If certain teachers had not played this role, I would not be who I am today.

We can find heroes among our elected officials. Many of them step up to take on the issues of our time with a belief that serving others is an honor, a privilege and a responsibility. United States Senator John McCain was an excellent example of this kind of person. His lifelong service always made him a superhero in my mind. There are many others – they can be found at all levels of government. This includes the service departments that offer support to the citizens of our towns, cities, states and our country.

And then there are the simple gestures expressed through ordinary actions by parents, friends, neighbors and even strangers. If we look at these actions as heroic, we can see how there are always heroes around us. We need to use this lens to see how much potential for good exists everywhere, all the time. We should never take this for granted.

Quantifying our Contributions: It all Adds Up

I once heard a student make this inspiring statement which has stayed with me for all these years:

> *"I read about a man who jumped from a train platform and saved a woman who had fallen on the tracks. He received an award for this and was honored in the newspaper. He deserved this recognition. What he did was amazing. But what about the little things? If a person does a thousand small kindnesses, doesn't it kind of add up to something like this? Can't we quantify our many good deeds in a similar way? Can't we demonstrate that big or small, all good deeds have value? And if someone was keeping track of them, we'd have a world full of superheroes out there. We need to honor and reward every good act. Not just the big ones. But all of them. Wouldn't this encourage more good? Wouldn't this result in a much better world?"*

This is an amazing statement. What if we could quantify our good and could keep score of all that is being done to help others? What if we could measure this good? These questions will be discussed in more depth in the *Care Points* and *Care Currency chapter.*

We all have Superhero Qualities

The previous statements outline the qualities of superheroes. Like them, you and I have the following characteristics:

- We have ups and downs and strengths and weaknesses.

- We understand the difference between good and evil and want good to triumph over evil.
- We would use whatever power and experience we have to help others when an opportunity arises.
- We care about this world; if asked to step up and help in a major crisis, most of us would.

It isn't the size of the heroic gesture; it is the heroic gesture itself. Big or small, it all makes a difference. Just offering our time makes us superheroes. We need to understand this and own it. In the words of the Yogi, Harbhajan Singh:

> "Life is a flow of love; your participation is requested. Our world needs more heroes. It is our job to bring out the hero that lives inside of each of us, making this world a better place."

7

WHERE THERE'S A WILL, THERE'S A WAY

What Motivates People to Step Up and Act?

Once in a while, amazing things are achieved when a large group of people spontaneously decide to take on the impossible. The circumstances that allow this to happen are not always well understood. But they offer an example of how humans can make a very tangible difference in addressing a problem when inspired. Here are several examples.

Indian Rape Case

In 2012, a 23-year-old female physiotherapy intern was beaten, gang-raped and tortured on a private bus in South Delhi. Eleven days after the assault, she was transferred to a hospital in Singapore for emergency treatment but died two days later from her injuries. This horrific incident generated national and international news coverage and was widely condemned in India and abroad.

Following this tragedy, massive public protests took place in New Delhi against the state and central governments for failing to provide adequate protection for women. Outrage broke out in other major cities throughout the country.

Since Indian law did not allow the Press to publish a rape victim's name, the victim was known as *Nirbhaya*, meaning "fearless", and her life and death came to symbolize women's struggles to end the rape culture in India. The public was accustomed to the long-held practice of denial of rape within the country, or otherwise blaming the victim rather than the perpetrator.

The protests resulted in the appointment of a judicial committee in December 2012 to take suggestions from the public regarding the best ways of amending laws to provide more rapid investigation and prosecution of sex offenders. After considering thousands of suggestions, the committee's report stated that failures by the government and police were root causes behind crimes against women. In 2013, several new laws were passed and six new fast-track courts were created to hear rape cases. Nirbhaya's case resulted in a tremendous increase in the public discussion of crimes against women. Statistics show that, as a result of these laws many more women have been willing to file a crime report.

A precedent case can create a viral movement that can bring about major changes. It is within the realm of possibility that public pressure to address a global issue could result from an incident that captures the world's imagination.

A Mine and a Cave

On August 5, 2010, there was a cave-in within the San José copper-gold mine, located in northern Chile. Thirty-three men were trapped 700 meters underground. To help rescue these men, exploratory boreholes were drilled. Seventeen days after the accident, a note was found taped to a drill bit pulled back to the surface, stating, *"We are well in the shelter, the 33 of us."* Three separate drilling rig teams, nearly every Chilean government ministry, the United States' NASA space agency and a dozen corporations from around the world cooperated to complete the rescue. On October 13, 2010, the men were winched to the surface one at a time, in a specially-built capsule, as an estimated one billion people worldwide watched. Private donations covered one-third of the $20 million cost of the rescue, with the remainder coming from the mine owners and the government.

In June 2018, a widely publicized cave rescue successfully extracted members of a junior football team trapped in Tham Luang Nang Non cave in Chiang Rai Province, Thailand. Twelve members of the team and their 25-year-old assistant coach entered the cave on June 23 after a football practice. Soon after, heavy rains partially flooded the cave, trapping the group inside. Efforts to locate the group were hampered by rising water levels and strong currents. For one week, there was no contact between victims and rescuers. Rescue efforts expanded into a massive operation, amid intense worldwide public interest.

On July 2, after advancing through narrow passages and muddy waters, two divers discovered the group alive on an elevated rock four kilometers from the cave mouth. Rescue organizers discussed various ways to extract the group. The rescue team pumped water for days before they could bring out survivors, as the next monsoon approached. Between July 8 and 10, the boys and their coach were rescued from the cave by an international team. These efforts involved more than 10,000 people, including over 100 divers, many rescue workers, representatives from around 100 governmental agencies, 900 police officers and 2,000 soldiers. It also required the pumping of more than a billion liters of water from the cave.

Sometimes a group of people who need help becomes such a phenomenon that no amount of money or manpower is spared. It is clear that extraordinary efforts can be put forward when the world decides it is important. These cases demonstrate that strong-minded, good-hearted people know that where there is a will, a way will be found. They also demonstrate that governments, NGOs, corporations and people from the general public can come together to bring about a united outcome. Finally, they show how a steadfast commitment to make something happen, no matter how dire the circumstances, can bring about a miracle.

Response to a Disaster

On December 26, 2004, a major earthquake in the Indian Ocean caused a devastating tsunami, killing an estimated 227,900 people in 14 countries. It was one of the deadliest natural disasters in recorded history. Indonesia was the hardest-hit country, followed by Sri Lanka, India and Thailand. Because of the widespread damage, a great deal of humanitarian aid was desperately needed. In the days that followed, huge numbers of responders addressed immediate and long-term aid for those who were suffering.

People from all over the world came together in unity to help address the problem at all levels – global, regional, national and community. The overwhelming need compelled people to act without hesitation. I was assigned to Sri Lanka for six weeks following the disaster and saw this response unfold in front of me. It was amazing to watch how many people volunteered to offer assistance. This was among the most dramatic of many similar disasters in other parts of the world.

Major disasters tend to unite people around an important cause; helping humanity in need. Having millions of people in forced labor situations is perhaps even more of a disaster. If we could find ways to treat them as human disasters, a united response should follow.

A Deadly Asteroid Coming toward Earth

We can speculate that other factors could result in collective action. What if scientists were to discover a massive asteroid heading toward Earth that would hit within a year? Knowing that a collision with such an object would cause an immeasurable catastrophe, the major governments of the world hopefully would come together to develop a viable plan. Even if it seemed as though the desirable outcome was completely impossible, they would do all in their power to address the unthinkable. While this scenario might seem remote, scientists say the Chicxulub impact, 66 million years ago, caused the extinction of the dinosaurs. In April 2018, the B612 Foundation reported, *"It's a 100 percent certainty we'll be hit by a devastating asteroid but we're not 100 percent sure when."*

This story is not new. In the 1998 movie, *Armageddon*, when an asteroid threatened to collide with Earth, NASA determined that the only way to stop it would be to intercept the asteroid in space, drill into its surface and detonate a nuclear bomb. Nine other movies on the subject have been produced.

What is the point of this? Obviously, as improbable as this whole scenario seems, many people fervently believe where there is a will, there is a way. Saving the Earth is a gloriously compelling motivation. What might seem like a completely impossible task would be put to the test. Everything science, technology and engineering had to offer would be explored and used. Knowing how resourceful mankind can be, I strongly believe an effective solution would follow. What if this same spirit of faith was applied to some of our major global issues? It is totally within the range of possibility.

On a Smaller Scale

Once in a while something happens that appears to present an insoluble problem. Years ago, I was driving my car along a remote

Nepalese road. The car stalled on a dangerous bend and could easily have been hit if a bus had come barreling around the corner. I managed to push my vehicle over to the curb to diagnose the problem but failed to see a deep ditch in front of me. Unfortunately, the front tire dropped into the ditch and the car stuck fast. I managed to re-start the engine but after several attempts I gave up trying to drive it out realizing that I needed a big truck to retrieve it. As I stood agonizing over my options, a local bus appeared, slowed down and stopped. Twenty men jumped out, gathered around my car and pushed it out of the ditch.

I hadn't flagged them down or called them over to help. It was quite simply a spontaneous and compassionate act. When finished, they climbed back on to their bus, waved goodbye and sped away. The whole thing took about six minutes. My head spun from this completely unexpected event that saved me untold hours of frustration. What happened? People in the bus saw my need and responded instinctively, expecting nothing in return. They performed this selfless act out of pure kindness.

Lessons Learned

The Indian rape case and the Thai cave rescue stories were dramatic enough to engage people worldwide in a passionate desire to see a good outcome. Equally tragic and widespread tragedies frequently go unnoticed. Most of us cannot imagine inhumane, brutal death-dealing events, which kill and destroy the lives of men, women, boys and girls. What is the difference?

First, the stories above made people see the need for immediate action. People would suffer and may even die. We see this with the mine and the cave narratives. There is a race against time. People regularly tune in for updates to see if something miraculous has happened. Curiosity and anticipation captivate the audience transfixed by the unfolding story. We all want to see what the final conclusion will be hoping for the best possible outcome. We root for this result.

Second, the size of the issues didn't overwhelm people because their scope was limited. The problem and response seem to have manageable boundaries. It is sometimes hard to get our minds around major global issues that seem so vast and expansive that the idea of helping seems unmanageable.

Third, problems like these have to be resolved within days or weeks at most, unlike major country, regional or global issues that will require years or even decades to resolve. We always see this following a major earthquake. The coverage continues until the declaration is made that the search and rescue operation is over. Then it stops.

Fourth, media and social networking coverage describing and promoting global issues and disasters enable each story to reach many people quickly. In the examples above, the problem rapidly became a conversation worth discussing. I remember being at my office and talking with colleagues about the Thai students in the cave. Everyone was worried about their health, whether they were still alive, and how they might be brought out, if found. The more people talked about this, the more people joined the collective conversation.

Fifth, the issues have to become personal. In both the mine and the Thai cave stories the media coverage described the victims and published and broadcast human interest stories related to family members and friends. In some cases, the heroic actions of the rescuers promoted the story further. We could see heroism unfolding before our eyes. We all felt inspired.

Whether a topic captures the public imagination is sometimes completely random. Many similar stories never materialize into more than a single column in a newspaper. Sometimes it is as if the stars align for a news story and then it becomes a phenomenon. It is completely hit or miss.

A Charismatic Idea

A story that goes viral is compelling and it inspires a desire to act. It is hard to know what creates this response but it is clear that these stories had some kind of charisma associated with them. Perhaps it was because they demonstrated that heroes, against all odds were going to rescue others in dire need. We wanted to believe it was possible. We wanted to see a miracle.

When a charismatic idea takes flight, it can spread everywhere. Two good examples of this include, "*Just say no*" and "*Only YOU can prevent forest fires*". These simple statements have captured the attention of many in a way that compels us to respond. During the First World War, the slogan "*I Want You*", on a picture of Uncle Sam, the personification of the US Government, pointing at us, encouraged thousands of people to sign up for the military.

As part of my own work, the "*Where Were You?*" story always produces a similar response. When Gita pointed at me and asked this question, it was an absolute epiphany. She was right. Where were we? Why weren't we acting on her behalf? Why didn't the world seem to care? The question itself is powerful because there is no reasonable answer. It forces us to think.

There is one TV commercial that I feel captures the essence of a charismatic idea. We see a man sitting on a chair mimicking driving. In slow motion, his head turns to the left to look at his wife and daughter who are sitting on a couch and smiling lovingly back at him. When he begins to turn back, his facial expression changes. You can tell he anticipates a collision. Before this happens, his wife and daughter run over to him. From behind, his daughter's arms wrap around his waist and his wife's arms go across his chest. Both are simulating seat belts. At the moment of impact, he kicks a tray full of confetti that shoots everywhere. This commercial helps the person watching it realize that you don't wear a seatbelt just for yourself, you do it for your family. The message was so well dramatized, it went viral.

We need more of these compelling ideas to bring about great breakthroughs. One way to motivate people's heroism is to inspire them. Charismatic ideas can hold untold potential for heroic outcomes.

What is the Point?

We need to learn from these events and try to find the magic formulas in these examples and replicate them. They demonstrate where there is a collective will, there is a collective way. Amazing, miraculous things can and do happen.

To me, many of the issues outlined in this book are slowly unfolding disasters. But they are disasters nevertheless. We all need to step up our game; we need to believe we can rise to many of these long-standing systemic challenges and we need to feel more urgency to act right now.

Why? Because we are not making any significant headway in addressing the major issues of our time and because every day millions of people suffering ask the question, *"Why is no one coming to help?"*

8

EXPANDING OUR HEARTS AND MINDS

A Parent's Love

I was inspired to write this section from an email I received from a mother. This woman wrote:

> "I only wish I could be a mom to those starving children. I wish I could give them the food and the love and the security they all need and deserve. Every once in a while, my heart seems to burst with love. I feel I have so much love in me I could save the world. I have had this feeling a few times in my life. I don't know where it comes from. I just know it is there."

Can you imagine if this was something we all felt? Can you imagine what our world would be like if we could all feel this love? Boy, would things be different.

Many of us are blessed with children. None of us get to choose who our biological children are but we love them nonetheless and take care of them because they are our own. They are our pride and joy and we love them deeply.

By contrast, all around the world, other children are born to parents in circumstances that are far less than ideal. Is it fair that some enter into loving, nurturing households, while others face severe poverty, disease, hunger, neglect and abuse? Of course not, but this is just the way life is for so many.

So, what if the love we feel for our own children could be expanded to include these poor children born into terrible situations around the world? Far too often, parental love stops at the boundary of our own homes. What if we removed these boundaries and allowed our compassion to spill out to those in need? Let's face it, if someone ever tried to hurt one of our children, as parents, we'd do everything in our power to protect them, wouldn't we? After all, our capacity for giving and receiving love is unlimited so why not share it?

To take this basic idea and apply it to the world would be heroic. Remember, heroism includes the process of overcoming almost impossible obstacles. Opening up our parental love to others is a huge task but one that is possible.

One more point – what would happen if we opened up our local paper and read an article about a 15-year-old girl from our own community who was commercially raped **7,000** times? How would we all react? There would be a collective uproar and we would demand action. Everyone would be asking, how can this happen, where is she, is she OK, what can be done? And yet, this outrageous tragedy happens every day to millions of girls and young women.

I am a father of two boys. I would do anything to protect them and would do the same for my wife, family and close friends. They are in my inner circle and I care about them. What if I could find ways to extend this circle to include these abused children? What if they became a real part of our own extended family? We can and should adopt them as our own.

Leaving Something Good Behind

Many of us want to leave an inheritance to our children. It is our final gift to them after we have passed away. This could include a house, a car, money, land or personal possessions. But what if there was something else we could leave to them – a safer, cleaner, more just, sustainable world.

At the close of a recent business meeting, the person I was with said:

> *"I woke up in the middle of the night and realized that the work I was doing related to health, safety and forced labor would help to make the world a better place for my kids and my grandkids. All of a sudden, I realized that this could be part of my inheritance to my offspring. I realized that my work had value beyond the pay check I received."*

Part of the reason for us to step up and be heroic is because of our love for our family and their future families. Many of the major crises the world will face will not affect most of us personally. By the time the full effects occur, we will be long gone. But when I think that my children and other future children, will face this hardship, I realize that I need to do something right now.

What if tigers and rhinos become extinct? What if more major storms hit the world? What if our climate completely changes? What if our air and water continue to become more polluted? What if we can't grow enough food to maintain the world population? What if America's national debt isn't addressed? What if racism isn't stopped? What if massive wild fires around the world continue to expand?

All of these factors will face both of my sons. Why do our kids need to bear the brunt of our mistakes and neglect resulting from us doing nothing? Why should they miss out and why should they suffer? Shouldn't we extend our legacy to include offering the best possible future for them?

Following a presentation I gave at a university in Hong Kong, a young Indian graduate student summed it up in this way:

> *"Why does society feel it is OK to pass on their junk to me? Why don't they realize that it will fall on my generation to clean up all their messes? There is no parent among them. Where is the compulsion to help fix these things? It just feels like people can't seem to see all of the bad things all around them. They are so selfish. This makes me feel sad. Your talk also made me feel angry at the world for being so irresponsible."*

As Albert Einstein once said:

> *"The world is a dangerous place to live; not because of the people who are evil, but because of the people who don't do anything about it."*

Failure to Act is Costly

In 2016, my wife, Sylvia and I organized a 70-day road trip across the USA and Canada to promote the issue of modern slavery. We visited 27 cities and made 114 presentations to corporations, schools, universities, faith-based groups and the general public. During this journey, at least a dozen people, mostly women, approached us and told us stories like this:

"I was at the bus station and I saw this man dragging a young girl along with him. There was something wrong about the situation. He wasn't her father. I could see that clearly. Part of me wanted to do something but I didn't know what to do. I still feel bad about that day. Maybe I could have helped that poor girl. I feel like I let her down."

There were at least ten variations of this same story. I found it disturbing just how similar these accounts were. Every person recalled the incident in great detail because they still felt guilt and shame.

Failure to act can have an impact on us, particularly when we know that someone is in trouble and something needs to be done. Regret can eat away at us.

Banking Heroes: Fighting Modern Slavery Through Compliance

In contrast to the previous stories, here is an example of what happens when a person does act. The feeling of accomplishment can have a lasting impact.

I once traveled to Washington DC to attend the American Bankers' Association Financial Crimes Enforcement Conference. As an anti-human-trafficking expert, I was invited to participate in two panel discussions focusing on the issue of modern slavery and the banking sector. Following the second session, one of the bankers told the following story:

"Three years ago, I was travelling with my wife and two daughters by car across several states in America to meet with relatives. Following a long drive, I pulled into a small motel for the night. That evening I went out to get some food for the family. Returning to the motel, I saw a young teenage girl pulled into a room by an older man. I remember she had such a sad, frightened expression on her face and suspected that she was a young prostitute about to be used by a patron. Since I had daughters of my own around the same age, I felt I needed to do something to help.

After dropping off the food, I went to the motel manager and told her what I had witnessed. I then returned to my room, not knowing if anything would happen. Twenty minutes later, there was a police car parked in front of the motel room. Ten minutes later, I saw a man being taken out in handcuffs. The young girl was escorted to another car and driven away. "

He said he remembered this event because he felt so good that he was able to help a young girl out of this terrible situation. Furthermore, he went on to say that this was a major milestone in his life – something he felt very proud of because he had taken action.

After hearing his story, I asked him what he did for a living. He said that he was a compliance officer focusing on anti-money laundering for a major bank. I asked him if his employer did any work related to the issue of modern slavery. He said the bank was just exploring what it could do in this area and that was why he came to the session. He went on to say that he felt his job was not very exciting and wasn't sure how much difference it was making.

Many People Help Unknowingly

People in banking compliance don't often realize that the outcome of their work has a major, positive impact on our society. Over the past two years, human trafficking has continued to emerge as an important issue within the banking sector. With an estimated US$150 billion generated from this illicit crime annually, banks must ensure that none of this illegal money makes it into their business. If it does and regulators find out about this, the bank can be fined for money laundering.

To address this issue, many banks across America are making major efforts to track this crime. They are training their employees; breaking down crimes into component parts to identify potential links with banking procedures (typologies); using "red-flag indicators" to search their data to find nefarious activities and, if found, sending this information to financial regulators.

Why is this relevant? Out of the 40 million people in modern slavery, the collective counter-slavery community helped rescue about 100,000 victims from this terrible crime last year. This means that with all of the NGOs, governments and UN organizations combined, only 0.2 percent of the victims were assisted. With banks becoming involved in the investigations, this could have a significant impact on the number of people helped.

With this in mind, I told the banker standing in front of me that while his day-to-day efforts might not seem as dramatic as his motel encounter, untold numbers of people would be assisted through his work in the coming years. I went on to say that those involved will be our future heroes because what they do will not only help to protect their bank, but also help to protect many other people like that teenage girl. Our job may seem such a small part of a puzzle but each part is essential.

Banks need to understand that by addressing the issue of human trafficking, they are not only protecting their business, they are also helping to address one of the most compelling injustices of our time. The outcome will be that many people will be freed from bondage. This makes their efforts TRULY HEROIC.

Feeling Guilty

Some people go through life with feelings of guilt related to the advantages they have been given. They feel that it is unfair that they have a comfortable lifestyle, while others struggle and suffer. This feeling rises to the surface when a person is exposed to global issues, especially the ones that affect vulnerable populations. Following many of my presentations, I witness this unfold:

> *"I feel terrible after listening to your talk. How is it that my life is so good and so many people suffer? I feel bad about this."*

> *"What can we do? Life is just unfair. But what am I supposed to do?"*

It has been my experience that people who decide to get involved in causes based on these criteria don't always make the best volunteers. Despite how it might sound, the reason for volunteering is basically selfish – to get rid of a person's guilt. Any motivation that is based on something like this is often not strong enough to maintain a sustained response.

> *"I got involved because I felt guilty. I felt compelled to do something."*

Research has shown that using individual guilt as a means of bringing about change doesn't work. No one likes to feel guilty about what they do or don't do. When people are reminded of this, many don't move in the direction of helping. Instead, they do what they can to avoid being exposed to these feelings.

For example, one of the major problems the counter-trafficking sector has faced is that the images are so graphic that people will do whatever they can to avoid being exposed to them.

> *"I know I should look at those kids on TV but I always turn away. I don't have the courage to look into their eyes. This always makes me feel guilty. Like I'm somehow letting them down."*

People should get involved in an issue because they want to help others, not themselves. Working to remove our guilt is helping ourselves.

What is the Point?

All of us love but most of us restrict our love to a finite group of people. If we could all open our hearts to more people, the collective response could really make a significant difference. All we need to do is bring about a mindset change.

Many people do heroic things as part of their regular work but don't make the connection. If more of us accept that our role adds value in blessing the world, perhaps this would incentivize us all to do even more. When we feel our work has value, or if we are rewarded for our efforts, we feel encouraged.

9

WHAT HAVE WE LEARNED?

Before exploring what can be done, it is important to summarize some of the major lessons learned related to the need for heroes and what holds us back. Here are some relevant insights we've discovered so far.

The World Needs our Help

As I noted in my opening chapters, our world is in trouble. Few of the efforts undertaken by governments, the United Nations and civil societies throughout the world come close to meeting today's urgent and overwhelming needs. Our usual methods can't solve the world's problems. We need massive campaigns that include the general public. We must raise individual awareness, advocate for change, enlist foot-soldiers to wage successful community campaigns and secure much-needed resources.

The vastness, complexity and depth of our global problems far exceed what any one set of organizations can address without help. We need to develop new partnerships, international collaborations and private/public partnerships.

We also need to find a way to allow all of us to play a role. With the world so well connected in so many ways, what we need now is strong, visionary leadership to help link all of the communities together. We need to accept this reality, own it and just get on with it. Every day of inertia is a day tragically lost.

Issues Choose Us

In the past, when I'd give a presentation on human trafficking, I'd try to get everyone in the room to feel just as passionate about the urgent human needs as I was. In reality, out of 100 people, only about 5 percent appeared to really care. The other 95 percent gave the impression that they had other issues on their minds.

What I have come to realize is that **we don't necessarily choose our issues, issues choose us!** What do I mean by this?

As I said earlier, I wasn't someone who wanted to become an activist but as I kept being exposed to the horrors of human trafficking, I became more deeply troubled by the topic. While working as a US public health official in Nepal, I was exposed to a full range of other very serious issues, including severe poverty, disease, illiteracy, racism and pollution but human trafficking was the subject which disturbed me the most.

Yes, I care about all of those other issues but not in the same way. There is something in me that is triggered by the idea of people, especially children and young people, losing their freedom. Others who share this same feeling have expressed it in a number of different ways:

> *"I don't know why it troubles me so much. It just does. I find myself being drawn to articles on trafficking. Of all the problems out there, this one seemed to creep up on me."*

> *"As a parent of daughters, I can't stand by and watch as girls, the age of my own, get abused this way. How can any parent allow this to happen?"*

Just as I am drawn to human trafficking, others find themselves being drawn to other problems. We all care about different things.

"Ever since I was a kid, I've wanted to help save endangered animals. One of my teachers told me that tigers might become extinct and right then and there I wanted to help. Tigers are such beautiful, majestic animals. Imagine if they were gone."

"I hate it that there are so many kids who can't read. I love reading. When I hear how many there are out there, I want to do my part. Reading is such a wonderful gift we should all share."

Why do some of us care about trees or whales or children or old people? It is because we are all wired differently. The sad thing is that most people do not take the time to find out what their cause might be.

I personally believe that many major efforts made by individuals fail simply because their heart isn't committed to a particular cause. I have had people volunteer for me who clearly cared more about another cause than the one I was managing. My advice to them is to give up the volunteer efforts with me and find a project that truly makes their heart sing.

Understanding that we all have a human cause that we care about deeply is a fundamental step in our journey to become heroic.

A Sense of Duty is Always There

I once read a newspaper article about a five-year-old boy who went missing in a small village in Scotland. Within one hour of his disappearance, nearly all the neighbors in the village gathered in a field near the child's home. Leaders came forward and pulled together a plan to search the surrounding forest. More than 600 people fanned out in every direction and began to call out the boy's name. Nothing stopped them – not the thorns, the thick brush, the insects nor the steep inclines. Each person accepted a role and played his or her part. Two hours later the child was found. He had become disoriented and wandered off in the wrong direction. The more he tried to find his way home, the more lost he became. They found him nearly two miles away. This time it was a happy ending.

People came together to help because they felt the parents' pain. They understood what it would be like to face something similar. No one had to explain the crisis. They felt it in their hearts. There was no question that everyone would drop everything. Their sense of duty was clear. This is what compassion is all about.

Compassion fuels our motivation. Finding a way to create an emotional connection with an issue is enormously powerful. We care because we can't stop ourselves from caring.

I have learned that finding ways to release a person's compassion is a fundamental part of the process of informing people. That is why heartfelt stories are so important and impactful.

Overcoming our Fears

One of the main reasons people don't get involved in addressing current issues is basic fear – fear of the unknown, fear of inadequacy, fear of failure and fear of criticism. Facing and overcoming our fears is the most successful way to set ourselves free. For many, it is the first step towards becoming a responder.

For much of my life, one of my worst fears was public speaking. These days I speak at around 150 public events each year. In the past, I would do anything to avoid this dreaded task.

I can trace the origin of this fear to an event that happened in the third grade. We were assigned to write three paragraphs about Abraham Lincoln. Since I was a student who often completed tasks at the very last minute, I took a shortcut and copied two long paragraphs directly from the encyclopedia. I felt confident despite my cheating.

When our papers were returned the next day, mine was marked unsatisfactory but that was not the end of it. My teacher asked me to stand up. When I did, she asked if the text I had written was my own. Of course I lied and said yes. She asked me again. I repeated the affirmation.

She told me to read my paper to the class. I knew I was in trouble and when I looked at the essay, I realized that I didn't understand many of the words I had copied down. Since the content was beyond my reading ability, I couldn't do it. Having no other choice, I began to read, often fumbling over many of the words. Every time I looked up at her, hoping she'd allow me to stop, she told me to go on. Clearly, she was making an example of me.

From that moment, I developed a terrible fear of public speaking. If I couldn't get out of a required speaking assignment, I spent days before the event with unrelenting fear and a multitude of mini panic attacks. Most fears, like mine, are based on an irrational criterion. But like many people, I allowed my fear to control me.

About ten years ago, I thought about the innumerable people who faced audiences every day. What was I so afraid of? Something had to change. I decided to face my fears because I had had enough of that fear controlling my life.

Finally, whenever presentation volunteers were needed, I stepped up. While my heart would say, "Don't do it", my mind took control. The process was not easy but something amazing happened. While I never eliminated all fear, my public speaking continued to improve. Now I realize that fear can be an important ingredient for a passionate speaker. Facing our fears may seem daunting but the payoff is incredibly valuable. Fear helps fuel my passion for a cause, inspiring my words and giving them more emotion and power.

Fear of change or the unknown must be addressed before we can really step into our role as a hero. Understanding this is an important part of our journey.

A banker I met at a conference offered a great insight that helped to put this factor into perspective:

> *"I am six feet tall and weigh over 250 pounds. I am a big person. Most people would look at me and think that I wouldn't be afraid of anything. But when it comes to change, I'm a big baby. I'm like that little boy who hides behind his mother's leg. I don't know why I'm so fearful of life and can't change direction."*

"Same" is Comfortable

Like all habits and routines, "same" remains comfortable. We know what to expect. As creatures of habit, we like the predictable. As we refine our likes, we also close out alternatives. Think about how you spend your weekends. Do you tend to do the same things, go to the same places and seek the same kind of entertainment?

For most of us, our days are mired in "sameness". What would happen if we had our coffee before taking our shower? What would happen if we got up 30 minutes later or 30 minutes earlier? What would happen if we drove a different way to work, listened to a different radio station, ate a different kind of breakfast or simply changed some aspect of our daily experience? By doing this, we would be changing the "same" routine.

Remember how it felt to begin a new job? We learned new things and experienced daily and weekly changes. In time, "new" was replaced with "same". The content of the meetings and activities might vary slightly but then sameness creeps in. In time, few things challenge us. Much of our work is done on autopilot. When we see this happening, it is time to make a move. Learning is a strong antidote to our "sameness" rut because it adds new insights, experiences and perspective of the world. Such opportunities are valuable.

Part of the reason why vacations are generally so special and enjoyable is that we eliminate daily routines. Experiment for yourself. Try an "upside-down day", changing everything about it. If you are thrifty, spend money. If you get up early, sleep late. If you eat healthy food, eat something delicious and fatty. This opens us up to "what if". What if I changed my life? What if I changed my habits and routines? Could things improve?

Why is this relevant? For most of us, getting involved in addressing the world's problems is not part of our "same." But like anything new, it has the potential to alter our lives, often in a good direction. However, for this new reality to occur, we have to take a chance and try new things having faith that the end-point will be positive.

Heroic action is a win-win situation. It is good for those we help and even more life-affirming for ourselves. It disrupts our "same" and feels great!

What Does it Mean?

All the ingredients needed to be a hero are already inside us. For some, a charitable nature is an integral part of who they are while others need to find the key that will unlock this part of themselves. Life becomes richer when we find our calling, overcome our fears and step into our full potential.

PART THREE:
SOLUTIONS

10

STEPPING UP

First Steps

We are all prepared to do heroic things. If you have done a kind, compassionate act for another, you have been heroic.

But we can do so much more. There are steps we can take to increase our heroic efforts. These can be used by people who are already actively involved in their chosen field as well as those who are just starting.

Decide, Accept, Surrender, Help - DASH

Acronyms can be used effectively to help us remember a set of statements in a particular order. The acronym I have come up with for the steps needed to ignite the hero inside of all of us is D.A.S.H:

- **D**ecide what makes your heart sing
- **A**ccept responsibility
- **S**urrender
- **H**elp

Why the word DASH? Synonyms for this word include rush, race, sprint and bolt. All express a sense of *immediate action*. Because each world issue discussed in this book requires an urgent response, I feel this acronym captures the right spirit. Second, another synonym for dash includes *plunge*. As a high school student once said to me:

> *"The only way I managed to join the club was to plunge headfirst into it. If I had taken the time to think about it, it never would have happened. It is best to close your eyes and just dive into the unknown."*

Step One: Decide What Makes your Heart Sing

Everyone has a cause that inspires them. We don't select our cause, the cause selects us. There is something about each of us that draws us to a particular topic – possibly because of who we are, our value system, our personal experiences or a combination of these factors. The subject of human trafficking chose me. In fact, I did everything I could to avoid engaging. I didn't feel I had the time but life seemed to conspire against me. Wherever I turned, this topic seemed to be in front of me – almost facing me down.

If you already know what your cause is, then you are ahead of the game. If you don't, the first step is to discover that cause. The process begins with a simple set of questions: "What is really important to me? What makes my heart beat faster? What would be my perfect job?" If you don't know, simply go online and read about various issues – it's easy. Alternatively, attend a lecture, read a book, watch a documentary or visit a developing country. Explore and try to learn and understand. As part of this process, I have had students say the following:

"I watched about a hundred YouTube videos. I cared about many topics but global warming was the one that kept coming back to me. This is the problem I am most scared about. Now that I know, I hope I can find something to do."

"I have always known that human trafficking is the cause that I want to help. Whenever I hear a story, I feel compelled to do something. I feel very passionate about this issue."

"I remember there was a point in her presentation when I said, 'Wow, this is pretty terrible.' I have to do something. It was like my mind was opened up to something that was already there. It was so powerful."

Understanding what connects us to a particular cause is essential. It allows us to fully commit. The more passionate we feel, the more we are inclined to help.

One of the biggest obstacles I have encountered among those who want to volunteer is the fact that they chose to address a particular problem that they didn't really care enough about. This mismatch usually results in an experience that is less than satisfactory.

"I spent six months volunteering for an organization that helped the homeless. It felt like work. While I care about these people, it just didn't excite me. I walked away feeling ashamed that I couldn't stick it out."

Getting to know who we are can help us all to better understand what our issue is and what we value. My journey through this process followed a series of distinct stages. I saw the horrific problem, felt a highly emotional response to it and knew I wanted to help and so I took appropriate action. Understanding what our compelling issue is must come first.

Step Two: Accept Responsibility

Responsibility is often hard to accept. It conjures up all kinds of scary concepts: duty, obligation, accountability and work. This is our world and it is our responsibility to heal and care for it. We can't control everything but we can definitely make a difference. Accepting responsibility is essential in helping to address our chosen issue.

Many of us take the world for granted. We take but we don't give back. Before we can give, we often need a reason. As noted throughout this book, the reason is simple. If we take from the world, we should always give something back. It is up to each of us to decide what we most want to contribute.

There is a hero in all of us. What we need to do is identify our heroic qualities and own them. One of my university professors summed this concept up succinctly:

> "We are all responsible for our life. It is ours to decide what we do and don't do. Many of us have countless choices we can make. At the same time, we also have responsibility to our world. We live in it. We benefit from it. We take from it. We are able to survive and thrive because of it. Because of all of these blessings we receive, we need to accept the responsibility to protect and defend it. If we don't, who will?"

When we see something we want to change in our world, we have the power to take action. We may not be able to stop horrible things from happening but we can raise awareness and help prevent them.

Each of us should stop and think about this basic question, *"How am I personally responsible for giving back to society?"* Taking the time to consider our answer helps us to better reflect on our own values. Below are some responses from people who have been asked this question:

> *"I know people say I should care about the world but I don't. There are people out there paid to solve our problems. Let them do their work. It is not my problem. I just want to live my life and be happy. There is nothing wrong with that."*
>
> *"I feel guilty that I don't do more. I know the world needs help. I realize this makes me part of the problem. I just don't know what to do."*
>
> *"Ever since I was in high school, I have tried to help. If we don't all do something, things will just continue to get worse. It is our civic duty."*

Not everyone feels the same sense of duty. I remember the moment I accepted responsibility for helping to combat human trafficking. A few days after I wasn't able to rescue Amulya, I was alone in my office and felt a strong desire to do something – anything. Knowing these girls continued to suffer every day, knowing there were virtually no programs in place to address this exploitation, knowing I had worked for a major development agency and knowing I had the means to act, I realized I needed to serve this cause. Once a person crosses this line, they make a profound, internal decision.

Many great people have emphasized the importance of taking responsibility. Below are a few quotes that I feel support this insight:

"There are two primary choices in life: to accept conditions as they exist, or accept the responsibility for changing them."

Dr Denis Waitley

"The purpose of life is not to be happy. It is to be useful, to be honorable, to be compassionate, to have it make some difference that you have lived and lived well."

Ralph Waldo Emerson

"Not for ourselves alone are we born."

Marcus Tullius Cicero

"Love is not patronizing and charity isn't about pity, it is about love. Charity and love are the same – with charity you give love, so don't just give money but reach out your hand instead."

Mother Teresa

"Doing nothing for others is the undoing of ourselves."

Horace Mann

Step Three: Surrender

When many of us hear the word *surrender*, we might think it is a negative concept. Surrender literally means, "*to give up or stop fighting*". However, there is another definition: "*submit to an idea or concept of service*". The person surrendering stops resisting thoughts and ideas that encourage them to get involved. Any natural tendency to resist surrendering to a higher good must yield to what we know is best for our world and ourselves.

After I crossed over the line and accepted responsibility to help, there were two paths I could follow. I could stop and think about it and risk talking myself out of this, or I could simply accept that a decision was made and own it. This third step focuses on turning our brain off, opening our heart and letting the question, *"What do I do now?"* unfold.

Not knowing what else to do, I finally surrendered. I accepted that, knowing what I knew about enslaved human beings and especially children, I could no longer turn away. I had to become fully involved and at that moment, an activist was born.

Many people who fight injustice have a similar story to tell. The reality of the pain and suffering gets under one's skin. Once absorbed, there is no escaping it.

We don't need to have such a dramatic story to motivate us. All a person has to do is say, *"I accept responsibility for a portion of the world's problems. I realize I have something to offer. I understand it is easy to walk away but will not do so. I am ready to do my part."*

This step requires a leap of faith, a leap into the unknown, a leap into a place where there might be hesitance, fear and uncertainty. In some ways, it is the breaking of our personal velleity. Our desire to move forward is fueled with a commitment to act. These comments reveal the essence of this milestone:

> *"After hearing what happened to those girls, I felt I could no longer turn away. Something inside me had changed. I knew I had to do something. There was no turning back."*
>
> *"I didn't understand what it means to surrender until I saw the picture of those animals in cages. They had suffered so much. They were skin and bones. How can people be so cruel? It made me cry. At that moment, I decided I wanted to help."*

People who think too much before they act often don't act at all. That is why surrendering is so essential – it takes this indecisiveness out of the equation.

Step Four: Help

Nike got it right when they came up with the slogan – *"Just Do It"*. It is a call to action, a challenge, a command and a commitment. When it comes to taking a stand and helping, a similar spirit is required.

At the end of all my presentations, I make the following statement: *"If every one of you did at least one thing – just one – this would add up to something great."* To illustrate my point, I show a picture of a massive sand dune in Cape Cod. *"These beautiful, natural structures, which seem to rise as high as the pyramids, are made up of billions of tiny pieces of sand."*

What is my point? Something great often comes from the accumulation of many small things. If everyone stood up and did at least one thing to add to the solution, a monumental outcome could be possible. There is great strength in numbers. Thus, if ten million people decide to act, this represents ten million steps forward.

After making this point, I then share a short list of easy-to-do activities that can be done with little or no effort. They include the following:

- Continue to learn about this subject and then pass this information on to your friends, co-workers and family through conversation or social media.
- Make a presentation or show a film at your organization, school, church, club or at a community event. This is relatively easy to set up.
- Be a responsible consumer. Many companies have statements on their websites regarding their environmental, labor and other policies that may impact your cause.
- Raise money or donate to the relevant NGO. A small amount of money to the right organization can really make a difference.
- Volunteer at a local organization. This can be done by working at a local NGO office, charity or at home by simply

doing Internet searches to collect information for your chosen cause.

Simple Acts of Heroism

Ordinary actions can be heroic. Some happen spontaneously, others are part of everyday life, while others require more effort. Examples include:

- A group of inmates at a California correctional facility volunteer to fight wildfires, at times risking their own lives. They offered this selfless work to help save communities in need.
- During TV coverage of Hurricanes Harvey and Irma, journalists spontaneously stopped reporting and began wading through floodwater to reach people in danger. They went from observing to responding because they felt they couldn't stand by and not act.
- Residents from surrounding states drove hundreds of miles to Houston to use their boats in rescue operations in the aftermath of Hurricane Harvey.
- A young woman in a long grocery line exchanged places with an elderly customer to put her ahead in the queue. Letting someone else go in front of us can seem like a simple gesture but it can be a great compassionate act of kindness.
- To encourage others to be healthier, a middle-aged man quit smoking, helping to convince people in his circle and his family to follow his lead. This action is heroic because it puts a person's desire to act as a role model ahead of his own habits.
- When the friend of a soccer team was saved by multiple blood transfusions following a car accident, members of the team visited a blood bank, donating their blood to show their gratitude to the people who saved his life. Giving blood is

simple and it feels good knowing that you could thereby save a life.

- A church leader encouraged each of the young people in his group to talk about themselves. For those who felt too shy to speak, he asked simple questions to encourage them to open up. Instead of skipping over them, he did his best to draw them out and build their confidence.
- A fourteen-year-old boy made a point of recycling everything he could throughout his day and persuaded his friends to do the same.
- A five-year-old child spontaneously picked up a piece of trash and placed it in a garbage bin.

After sharing these examples with a friend, they made the following comment.

> *"What you are doing is not right. According to this list, nearly everything a person does that is considered helpful in some way is heroic. Heroism has to be more than this. It has to require some kind of bravery or sacrifice."*

I completely disagree. There are not enough positive, supportive, helpful gestures offered in our everyday life. When something good is done to help a person, an animal or the planet, it should be rewarded, it should be valued, it should be recognized. It is heroic.

Formalize your Commitment

For years, I have been asking audiences to do things to help address a particular issue. After making this request, I came to realize that few people ever followed through. Why? Because they hadn't formally committed to do something.

With this in mind, I decided to change my approach. Now and then, at the end of a talk, I ask those people who want to get involved to stand up. Usually everyone stands up. Peer pressure requires we do this or we might be judged as not caring. I then ask them to repeat a statement if they wish.

> *"I, (state your name), agree to do at least one activity a year that will help contribute to the fight against modern slavery."*

While the result of this pledge does increase the number of people who actually do take action, I then took it one step further. After getting people to stand up, I then asked them to repeat this statement.

> *"I, (state your name), agree to do at least one activity a year that will help contribute to the fight against modern slavery. I will send an email to Matt Friedman indicating what I will do and provide an update when I have done it."*

While the result of this pledge increased the number of people who actually did take action, I wanted to see if I could get even more. So when a person sends me an email, I ask them to read this statement, print it out and then sign it:

> *"I, (state your name), agree to do at least one activity a year that will help contribute to the fight against modern slavery. With my signature below, I am committing myself to act. This is an agreement with myself to follow through."*

For some reason, this approach appears to work best. Printing out the document and signing it really motivates a person to act.

> *"After I signed my contract, I put it on my refrigerator. Every time I go to get something out, I see it there in front of me. This reminds me that I committed my time to something worthwhile."*

If you are ready to commit and to act, I encourage you to take this step. If you want to go even further, you can list the actions you plan to take and sign your name to this.

If a person follows the DASH formula, they are on the way to a heroic life. If everyone accepted this challenge, imagine where the world would be.

11

HOW TO DO GOOD

In his inaugural address, John F. Kennedy spoke these famous words, *"Ask not what your country can do for you; ask what you can do for your country."* I would like to suggest a slight re-wording of this quote to read, *"Ask not what your world can do for you; ask what you can do for your world."*

This chapter will offer some simple suggestions on how to get started. This is by no means an exhaustive list. There is a wealth of amazing, evolving information available on the Internet that goes far beyond this description.

Individual Contributions

Each of us has our own way of doing things. Some of us like to be part of an organization or campaign while some would rather work on their own. Whatever your preference, I suggest you go through the DASH steps. Once you have decided on your issue, accepted responsibility, surrendered and agreed to help, it is time to take action. The list of things that a person can do as an individual is endless. Here are a few suggestions:

- Share relevant articles and stories about your chosen area of interest on your social networking platforms.
- Send letters to encourage public officials to address a particular community issue.

- Raise money through your network and donate it to a worthy cause.
- Write an article for the local paper offering your opinion and insight about a public problem.
- Be a positive role model in your daily life to others who are interested in a given issue. For example, if you want to address global warming, reduce your carbon footprint and encourage others to do the same.

It is up to us to decide what to do. Many websites offer similar lists that encourage a person to get involved. Googling can be another effective way to generate ideas.

Make a Plan

One way to ensure that you complete the activities you set out to do is to develop a simple schedule and plan. I find I am more likely to achieve results when I make a "to-do list".

There is something about seeing a list in a notebook or on a screen that urges a person to act. It seems more official and real. Once you complete each task, you can cross it off. Over time, your list begins to look really impressive. These small, heroic actions can be a source of great encouragement.

> "I started tracking my volunteer activities over five years in my journal. When I look back at these achievements, I feel really pleased. I actually did a lot of cool things."

I sometimes tell others of my plan and ask them to check in on me to ensure I follow through. These people keep me encouraged and accountable. This can also be a two-way arrangement, whereby both parties agree to ensure the other achieves their goals.

Using our Personal Gifts

Each of us has at least one gift – something at which we excel. It could be art, music, drama, poetry, dance, singing, planning, managing, designing or being creative. We thrive when we apply these gifts to our heroic efforts. Over the years, I've seen this principle applied many times in the human trafficking sector:

- A nine-year-old artist created paintings of Kung Fu Panda going after trafficking victims. These paintings were printed on a postcard to raise money for local NGO activities.
- A high school student choreographed an interpretive dance depicting a trafficking scenario in India. She taped the dance and disseminated it through social networks to raise awareness.
- A middle school student developed a short film to show the relationship between modern slavery and supply chains. It is so effective that the United Nations continues to post it on their website.
- A professional singer wrote a song that depicted the plight of women in sex slavery. A music video based on the song was eventually produced.

Combining what we are good at with a social issue can be a win-win on both fronts.

> *"I chose to do dance because that is what I excel at. It was meaningful to combine my two passions."*
>
> *"I never thought I could draw and use this to help children. It's as if God wanted me to bring these two parts of myself together."*

Form your own Group

Some people identify a few other like-minded individuals and start their own working group. The advantage of this approach is that it is easy for the members to maintain control of what they do and they don't fall under an organization's hierarchy. As part of this approach, the group discusses and debates what they will do together. Over the years, I have seen this work well. Examples include:

- Setting up a screening of a film on climate change to help communicate this message to others.
- Canvassing a neighborhood to promote the adoption of abandoned animals.
- Making and selling handicrafts at a holiday bazaar to raise money for a charity that supports children.
- Handing out pamphlets on poverty alleviation at a mall to help raise awareness.
- Looking for homeless people on the streets to refer them to shelters.

One of the advantages of this approach is that it helps develop a spirit of camaraderie. This team spirit can be very satisfying and, in some cases, even inspiring. As team members encourage each other and combine their individual talents, uncertainty and self-doubt are replaced by confidence. A collective sense of accountability is also built into the process.

> *"I never would have done anything if my friends didn't join me. I have a bad habit of starting things and then just stopping. When they are around, they kick my butt and I'm much better."*

Participation When Requested

Another approach is to sign up as a volunteer for an organization. Sometimes, these groups call on volunteers to help for a given period of time. Once the task has been completed, there might not be another request for weeks or months. Organizations that use this approach often have fluctuating volunteer requirements, depending on their annual needs. The advantage of this way of working is that it takes up less time and can be based on a person's own schedule. Examples of these programs might include:

- Selling T-shirts from a booth at a concert
- Participating in a "fun run" to raise funding
- Helping with the logistics of a fundraising gala
- Stuffing envelopes for a mass mailing campaign
- Making calls to businesses to raise community awareness

Long-Term Commitment

Some make a commitment to join an organization as an intern or volunteer. In this case, the commitment is much more substantial. Often such programs advertise an opportunity, interview potential candidates and then agree on a set of specific tasks. In other cases, a person simply reaches out to an organization to offer their services.

Within my own organization, most of our volunteers offer their support without a request being made. Our approach to having volunteers or interns is simple – we either further develop their specific skill sets or help them learn new ones. We want each person to be satisfied with their assignment.

Over the years, I have had mixed results with volunteers. As noted throughout this book, people take on these roles for a number of reasons: out of guilt, peer pressure, a desire to give back or a resumé booster to help get a job or a university placement. Our motivation most often determines the ultimate outcome. Knowing this, I do as much as I can to ensure that their commitment will be genuine and will be honored. Reasons for dropping out often include:

- An impulsive decision was made without realizing the amount of time required
- A person volunteers for something that does not fit their skill set
- The tasks assigned did not sufficiently interest them
- The activities they were asked to do were beyond their abilities
- The individual didn't take the assignment seriously because they were an unpaid volunteer and didn't value the work

Some of my best jobs resulted from volunteer positions I accepted at different stages in my life. As an undergraduate, I took an internship with an oncology lab at a major teaching university. After a year of volunteering, I was hired for the remaining four years. When I was getting my master's degree at New York University, I interned at the United Nations. After completing this assignment, they began hiring me to do regular consultancies. That set the foundation for my career in international development.

My advice to those who volunteer is simple – put in 150 percent, learn as much as you can, offer to help whenever you can and make yourself indispensable. This is especially important if you are interested in using a volunteering activity to transition into a career choice.

Learning from our Own Heroes

One of the best ways to become a hero is to learn from those who have been heroic throughout their lives. Four of my biggest heroes happen to be related to me. While all of my family members have their own unique gifts and special qualities, some of them have been more heroic, based on the way they chose to live their lives.

From the time I was a small child, my mother volunteered her time. I grew up watching her be heroic nearly every day. One day she'd collect money for the National Cancer Society, the next day she'd help the Boy Scouts prepare for an overnight trip and then she'd be shoveling snow off an elderly neighbor's driveway. When it came to helping others, I don't think she ever used the word "no" because serving was a core value of hers. While I often complained when she forced me to participate in her many voluntary activities, I realized that these efforts helped set the foundation for my own involvement in public service. She showed those around her what a "life lived good" was all about.

My father dedicated his entire adult life to studying and predicting the impact of natural disasters on communities. Always a pioneer, he never shied away from what was needed to understand an issue. When others would say, *"We need more data"*, my father would continue to work with what he had. His innovation and insights helped to build a foundation for the benefit of the whole insurance industry, changing the way they looked at their business and their responses. Without knowing it, he helped untold thousands and even saved many lives. He was also one of the wisest persons I have ever met. One of his most enduring comments, which has stayed with me, was: *"Pure genius is when a person is able to take the most difficult and complex topics and make them understandable to an eighth grader but also have them be beneficial to a PhD."*

My sister Carrie is the most dedicated person I have ever met. From childhood, she has cared for and loved every animal that came into her world. When she was older, she translated this innate passion for animal rights into her NGO entitled "Out-to-Pasture." Her mission is to take broken, abused and mistreated animals who are suffering and heal them. While the world has a way of disposing of such creatures,

Carrie believes they all deserve the right to a full and satisfying life. With nearly 45 cats, 45 dogs, horses, goats and sheep, she cares for these animals 24/7 – feeding them, treating them, diapering them and comforting them. It consumes much of her life. Even with their ailments and disabilities, these animals appear happy and fulfilled. When I look at Carrie's commitment, it almost makes me feel like I am a slacker. As each disabled animal grows older and eventually dies, she mourns. I always felt this unconditional love for animals is what spurs her on and is at the heart of her committed activism.

And finally, there is my wife, Sylvia. From the first day I met her, she demonstrated a spirit of compassion and justice. I met Sylvia on her first day as a documentary producer for a major TV channel based in Hong Kong. She was producing a series of films on the issue of human trafficking in different locations, including Hong Kong, Thailand, Cambodia and China. On the day she was supposed to interview me, I was very sick. I told her I had to give a talk at the American Chamber of Commerce but I couldn't do her interview as well. I suggested that she come to the Chamber talk and shoot what she could. When she arrived, she walked over and handed me some medicine. This act of kindness and care for my well-being from a complete stranger stayed with me. There are few people I have ever met who have more of a sense of justice. If a person was being oppressed or abused, she'd do everything in her power to help. If a documentary was needed, she'd make it. If a book was required, she'd write it. If a program needed to be set up, she'd recruit the people and make it happen. On many occasions, her sense of duty inspired me to carry on doing what I was doing.

Each of the people above have lived heroic lives and their unwavering commitment has provided a role model for me and many others. Over the years their heartfelt actions and behavior influenced me greatly. We can learn much from people who play such roles in our own lives and I feel grateful for those who served this purpose in my life. I know I am a better person today because of their inspiration, insight and mentoring.

Major Sporting Events: Lessons Learned

Now and then I attend a live sporting event. I'm always impressed by the level of enthusiasm shown by fans who are engaged and excited for many reasons.

- Sport offers individuals an opportunity to feel like winners when their team does well. They share in the victory because they feel they are part of the team. This boosts their self-esteem.
- People engage in the drama that goes along with a team's struggle to succeed.
- The immediate outcome is uncertain and unknown. Since anything can happen, we want to watch and participate because we have a yearning to see our team win.
- Often life seems ordinary and uneventful. Sporting events can help to fill this void with action and excitement and provides escapism.
- A good match offers an opportunity for team members to be heroic. Some people live vicariously through their athletic heroes. It inspires them to follow their lead.
- A sporting event allows a person to enthusiastically express themselves as the game unfolds. Where else can you stand, shout and cheer like this?
- It offers a sense of belonging. It is one of the few times when people come together with a common cause – to root for their chosen team.
- If a team is an underdog, it allows the audience to cheer for them. Any team that overcomes obstacles to win inspires us and offers a sense of hope.

When I watch 100,000 people standing, cheering and showing their extreme passion, I sometimes wonder if there is a way to tap into this energy, excitement and longing to be a part of something. Could we motivate people to get just as excited to support global causes?

Imagine how much more we could do if this massive collection of emotion could be harnessed to achieve good. Why not? Has it ever been tried?

Using Competitions: a Motivating Factor

Competition encourages innovation. It motivates people to step up and give more of themselves. We all want to be winners. It feels good. Achieving adds to our self-esteem and self-worth. People who compete as a group unite in a common purpose.

Many examples of heroism can show up in competition, as I've listed below. They may be small, but offer hope for the trend to increase.

Hackathons: A hackathon is an event in which a group of people with different skills, including computer programming, software development, graphic design, interface design and project management, come together to solve a social issue using technology. Different teams compete to see who can come up with the best idea. Hackathons allow us to try out our crazy ideas. They encourage us to think outside the box. Because the process is done within a team setting, it allows people to engage creatively. If an idea does not work or can't be operationalized, such failures are low cost.

> *"Within one day we designed a new App to solve the problem. I learned so much from the people in my group. It just goes to show that when people put their heads together, great things can follow."*

Strategic Planning Wars: There is another approach within the development community that also uses competition as a foundation. A workshop methodology entitled "Strategic Planning Wars" is used to create a project design. This is how it works:

- Approximately 20 voluntary experts within a given sector are identified and divided into two teams.
- The same development problem is offered to each group. During the two-day workshop, each team works to come up with a project design to address the problem. The workshop represents an academic competition, or a strategic planning skirmish.
- At the end of the second day, each team presents their design to a panel of three expert judges, who determine the winner. An audience of their peers is also invited to attend the big reveal.
- The winning team is selected and receives an award. The winning design is used to address the development issue.

This kind of friendly competition helps to keep people focused; uses a team's ego to get 120 percent from each person in order to win; develops a sense of teamwork that will be sustained throughout the entire workshop and makes the event interesting, innovative and fun.

> "I'm so glad I attended. During most workshops, by the second PowerPoint presentation, I'm tuning out and doing emails. I get so bored. This methodology compelled me to work as hard as I could. I wanted to win. I also made some new friends."

Using Competitions to Highlight our Creative Skills

I have been involved in school and church-based competitions to see who can come up with the best film, song, painting, essay or poetry related to a given issue. In each of these cases, the artistic discipline allows people with immense creativity to use their gifts for good. The winner's work is then promoted through a range of public networks to raise community awareness. Since each of us relates to our world in a different way, some of these unique approaches can have an impact where others have failed.

> *"I am a music guy. When that song was sung, wow, the message really hit home. Give me a good song over a docudrama any day. That is what does it for me."*

These approaches represent new, effective, pioneering, heroic ways to get results in a short period of time. By understanding and utilizing basic human nature through this process – our competitiveness, our ability to work collaboratively and our ability to do things in a limited amount of time – we can continue to evolve as practitioners in our respective developmental sectors.

Political Rallies and Concerts

Political rallies offer a similar form of collective participation. These events allow candidates to share their policies and raise support during election campaigns. In a big political race, the crowds drawn to these events can be massive. While most candidates talk about the good they will do, it is they who are the center of attention. Isn't it great when the issue is the center instead?

One good example is the 1985 Live Aid concert set up to raise money for the famine victims in Ethiopia. This concert was held simultaneously at Wembley Stadium in London, UK, (attended by 72,000 people) and John F. Kennedy Stadium in Philadelphia, USA, (attended by more than 100,000 people). It was one of the largest televised events in history, reaching 1.9 billion people in over 150 countries. This means nearly 40 percent of the world participated. Over US$150 million was raised. Thousands of volunteers participated all over the world to enable this to happen.

"Being a part of that concert was one of the highlights of my life. I felt proud of everyone who stood beside me shoulder to shoulder. Everything was electrifying. It blew my mind."

On December 16, 2012, I attended an event in Myanmar, in which an American Pop singer, Jason Mraz, gave a concert to raise awareness of human trafficking. He was the first foreign artist to play an open-air concert in this once isolated country. The concert was organized by Walk Free and the MTV EXIT campaign. In a country where no more than five people were allowed to congregate, watching 70,000 people come together to learn about human trafficking was an amazing experience. Having visited Myanmar 25 times prior to this event, witnessing a nation evolve in this way brought tears to my eyes.

The world needs more of these events. Anyone watching the footage of these epic concerts can see that those who participated were as excited, engaged and passionate as spectators at any major sporting event. This demonstrates that mass actions can be used to bring about change.

Great Spontaneous Ideas

Sometimes we are standing in our shower and suddenly, we have a very interesting, innovative idea. When these ideas help us to address our global problems, something amazing happens. The difference between a great idea and a great achievement is when someone decides they will make it happen. This, by its nature, is heroic. Here are a few simple examples:

Adopt-a-Highway Program: Volunteers adopt a stretch of highway to keep it free of litter and their name is posted on a sign to recognize their efforts. The idea for this program originated in the 1980s when James Evens, an employee from the Texas Department of Transportation, saw some garbage fly out of a car on the highway.

He sought local volunteers to clean up the roads because it was too time consuming and expensive for the town government. A national program developed from this idea. As a result, many of America's major highways are pristine and beautiful.

Using Discarded Plastic Bottles to make Roads: Realizing that plastic waste was a major problem for landfills, innovators in the UK and India experimented with melting and adding the discarded plastic to asphalt to see if this would result in better roads. The idea worked and we now see this technology being used in Australia, Indonesia, India, the UK and the US. This novel idea brings recycling and construction together to create roads that show better wear resistance.

Water is Life Project: A researcher at Carnegie Mellon University developed an amazing, low-cost education and water filtration tool – a book in which each page is a water filter. Each page provides water and sanitation advice, for example, the importance of keeping rubbish and faeces away from water to avoid contamination. Once the information has been read, the page is pulled out and used to purify water, reducing harmful microbes. Each book has enough filters to provide the reader with clean water for up to four years. This simple, cost-effective tool is being used throughout Asia, Africa and Australia.

All of these amazing ideas have helped to improve our world and benefit people across the globe. Imagine if we could encourage more and more people to be involved in applying their unique, innovative ideas to the issues of our time. The sky is the limit.

What Does it all Mean?

Each of us needs to decide how we want to be heroic. We can do it alone, as part of a group, within an organization or within a business.

Once we have decided to get involved, we can make appropriate choices. To help with this process, there are countless videos, articles, blogs and exposés on the Internet that offer everything we need to begin. This chapter highlights a few of these options. I encourage you to dive in and begin your own heroic journey.

12

THE BENEFITS OF BECOMING A HERO

Payback from Doing Good

I often encounter people who equate volunteer work with sacrifice and drudgery. It conjures up visions of mindless, repetitive activities that are boring and tedious. However, being heroic through our charitable actions and deeds benefits us in many ways.

Mental Health Benefits

Research has demonstrated that when we contribute to charity in some form, the *nucleus accumbens* within our brain is triggered. This part of our brain processes our pleasure and reward responses. When we give or contribute, our mind and body are wired to feel good. Our brains begin to spark in ways that allow us to feel euphoria, joy and a winning spirit. Thus, we can find happiness simply by being generous with our time, money and efforts.

> *"Most people don't understand when I say this but I'm addicted to my environmental work. I sometimes find myself getting a massive rush from our campaigns. It's like a drug."*

I have offered volunteer support throughout much of my life. Some of my happiest and most fulfilling moments came about during times when I was helping others. While I always thought this resulted from simply feeling good that my contributions made a difference, perhaps there was something more – a shot of dopamine and serotonin in my blood.

It Fulfills our Need for a Purpose

Many of us seek a sense of purpose. While some of us can find meaning in our jobs, within our family or among our friendships, others need more. Doing heroic deeds can fulfill this desire. Our achievements can fill a void and offer personal satisfaction by offering direction.

> *"After I retired, I began to feel bored and useless. I didn't know what to do with all my time. I wanted to pull my hair out. The volunteer work I did at the children's ward changed everything. I once again had a purpose. I began to feel valued."*

> *"Since I was a kid, I knew what my purpose was. I was one of the real lucky ones – I always had a straight path. Some of my friends are in their late sixties and still can't answer this question."*

If you have ever felt your life lacks purpose, when this void is filled, you will often experience a transformation. The imbalance described earlier can be corrected by getting involved in a worthy cause. It can truly be a life-changing experience.

> *"There was the me before I joined that club and the me after. My soul went from rags to riches. It gave me a new lease on life."*

Our Efforts Impact Others

As Rod Siltanen once said, *"The people who are crazy enough to think they can change the world, are the ones who do."* Dr Margaret Mead went on to say, *"Never doubt that a small group of thoughtful, committed citizens can change the world. Indeed, it is the only thing that ever has."* Imagine what a large group can do.

If we compare our world now to what it was a hundred years ago, we can see some miraculous changes. The rule of law is better and more universal. People no longer die from famine and hunger on such a major scale. Diseases that once killed millions are being cured. Human rights declarations offer a template for what is just and what is right.

Many of these advancements resulted from an individual or a group of people who took it upon themselves to research, advocate and change the way things were. While many of you reading this book may feel that your contribution is simply a drop in a bucket, all of these drops are needed to fill that bucket. Every drop has impact. Every drop has meaning. Every drop is necessary. Never, ever doubt that any kind, compassionate, selfless gesture will make a difference. It all adds up.

Within the anti-slavery sector, William Wilberforce offers a good example. During the 18 years between 1789 and 1807, he did everything in his power to lobby and persuade the UK's House of Commons to enact legislation to free slaves throughout the British Empire. Despite the lengthy period of time, he finally succeeded.

Who will be the next Wilberforce in addressing racism, terrorism, disparity, poverty and the like? Maybe it will be you. Some of the activists I most admire in this world started as teachers, mothers and administrators. They took it upon themselves to join a cause and then blossomed. Their latent leadership came alive and prospered. These people had no idea that ability was in them. It only began to grow when they opened themselves up to change.

It Builds Relationships

Research tells us that one of the outcomes of modernity is isolation, loneliness and a lack of community. Face-to-face interactions are being replaced with face-to-screen interactions. Loneliness can have a wide range of physical and emotional health impacts, including depression, substance abuse, cardiovascular disease and increased stress levels.

I read an interesting article that illustrated this trend. A young man named Carl had more than 500 friends on Facebook. Hoping to celebrate his appreciation for his online community, Carl invited them all to a party at the park. Since most of his Facebook friends lived close by, he expected that at least half would attend. When the big day arrived, only four people showed up. You can imagine his shock and surprise. While we may think that our social network community represents something real and tangible, in many ways, these relationships are often very superficial and meaningless.

Many volunteering and campaign opportunities allow us to come together as a group or community. This allows our face-to-face interactions to increase and flourish.

> *"Before joining the charity, I felt so lonely. I now have a group of people I work with who I care about and they care about me. My life is so much better."*
>
> *"The people I volunteer with have become my sisters and brothers. I love them all. I can't imagine my life without them."*

Getting involved in a cause allows people to break out of isolation. People who share the same interests can come together in unity to achieve a common goal – to help the world. In my own case, some of my closest, lifelong friends come from my volunteer circles.

Personal Growth

Throughout the literature, many studies highlight a direct link between our heroic actions and our personal growth. There is something about giving of ourselves that brings joy, happiness and a desire to do more. We are changing and expanding our experiences because we find ourselves growing through our successes and failures. Thus, helping others can offer the secret ingredient to living a productive, pleasurable and meaningful life.

I have also seen how volunteering can help to develop both confidence and self-esteem. In a world where these characteristics are often lacking, volunteering can bring about amazing transformations. I have often repeated this phrase, *"Those who do heroic acts often get more out of the experience than those they serve."* In the best of circumstances, both benefit equally.

> *"Working with victims of human trafficking helped me to grow up inside. I realized that I was kind of immature. I became humble and more sympathetic."*
>
> *"I had an eating disorder for years. After volunteering at my church, all of that stuff stopped. I stopped looking at me, me, me."*

Being heroic changes us. It forces us to see the world in another way. It enables us to think about others instead of just ourselves. It gives us new experiences that challenge us, test us, humble and awaken us. This all helps to open us up to a completely different life experience.

What Does it Mean?

Helping others can be good for us. It can give us confidence, boost our self-esteem, expand our skills and experience and even make us healthier. H. Jackson Brown sums this up nicely with this quote, *"Remember that the happiest people are not those getting more, but those giving more."*

13

CARE POINTS AND CARE CURRENCY

Quantifying our Contributions

In Chapter 6, I posed the question, *"If a person does a thousand small kindnesses, shouldn't this add up to something?"* Is there a way to take our heroic gestures and quantify them?

Recognition and Feeling Valued

The world seems to value certain aspects of a person's life more than others. We are interested in the amount of money a person makes, the size of their home, the car they drive, the position they hold in a company and the education they have achieved. These things somehow prove whether a person has lived a good, successful life.

Another thing that we seem to focus on are the bad things that happen in our world. In fact, much of our media infrastructure appears to be based on this emphasis. News seems to focus almost entirely on negative issues. Good news often translates as "no news". Do we not care about the good things that happen around us? Most people do and I certainly do.

If we focus on the bad, we need to balance the equation with something that highlights the good. Let me offer some examples:

- Yes, the world is helping less than one percent of the victims of modern slavery but governments, NGOs and community groups are all learning about the issue and setting up their own programs to address it.
- Yes, there is global warming but a growing number of university, private sector, government, United Nations, corporation and community efforts are being set up to respond to the problem. The collective impact of all this work is tangible.
- Yes, animals like elephants and tigers have become endangered but at the same time there are people who risk their lives every day to protect them.

Good deeds, in their myriad forms, are happening all around us. On an institutional level, this kind of work is often measured and tracked. We can get a relative picture of what is being done and what is being achieved.

But what about individual contributions? How do we track the impact of volunteers and interns that help in this process? How do we measure the goodwill offered by ordinary people? Until recently, this process has never been standardized. So, what if there was a way we could track the good? What if we could accept that good deeds are relevant and important and deserve some kind of recognition? What if we could measure them the way we measure so many other things?

Care Points

A care point is a numeric score assigned to an activity that addresses a social problem. People earn points by doing good things. For example, if a person watches a documentary on hunger in the United States, they receive two care points. If they set up a community screening of the film, they get five care points. If they volunteer for ten hours at a local food bank, they get eight care points.

The points are based on a sliding scale – the more relevant the action is to a solution, the more points are offered. The purpose of this approach is to quantify and standardize the efforts being made by people who get involved in a cause. The more they do, the more points they receive. This approach is based on the honor system.

In Hong Kong, this care point concept is being tested for the first time to address the modern slavery issue with the help of the *End Slavery App*. Participants are awarded care points for every action they take. How does this work?

- The participant downloads the free *End Slavery App*
- The participant signs up to be an anti-slavery responder (providing their email address)
- The participant chooses "*Activities*" from the "*Take Action*" menu and follows the instructions. There are nine categories to choose from to join the fight: learn, share, teach, be creative, volunteer, give, report, encourage and be responsible. Within these categories there are 37 activities to choose from
- For each action taken, the person earns care points to monitor their progress. According to the calculations, it is estimated that 50 care points significantly contributes to the rescue of a person in modern slavery
- Every participant is encouraged to get others involved

While this App presently focuses on addressing human trafficking, the concept of care points could be expanded to include any action taken to address a cause – global warming, pollution, bullying, racism, animal rights, etc.

Why is Recognition Important?

Over the years, I have asked many volunteers, *"What was the most positive thing about your experience?"* The most common response was, *"It felt good to be able to help address the problem."* The second most common response was, *"It felt good to be recognized and valued."*

When we posed the question another way: *"What was the most negative thing about your experience?"* the answer was often, *"I didn't receive much recognition for my contribution."* Clearly, recognition and being valued is considered important. Below are actual comments from volunteers:

> *"I spent nearly three months volunteering for that charity. But at the end of the project, I didn't even receive a simple thank you. I felt this was kind of disrespectful. I felt used."*
>
> *"I would have done more to support the cause but I really didn't feel they appreciated all the time I spent. A simple email would have been nice."*

For years, market research has confirmed that some form of recognition or reward motivates people to maintain and expand their involvement in activities. Without this, many people rapidly lose interest. This is one of the reasons why Facebook has been so successful, the "like" tab offers instant recognition for our posts and this motivates people.

Any form of gratitude can go a long way. Expressions of appreciation can foster strong, collaborative ties and pave the way for more continued involvement in community efforts. Simply thanking a person for work completed can lead participants to be twice as likely to continue volunteering.

Ways that gratitude can be expressed include a thank-you email, public recognition at an event, a smile, a handshake and so much more. All of these gestures trigger that part of our brain that makes us feel good and happy.

One other way to honor heroes is to reward them with a prize. All over the world, there are ceremonies where medals, certificates and awards are offered, sometimes for an act of courage, other times for a program or a lifelong contribution. Major global awards include the Nobel Peace Prize, CNN's Annual Hero Award and the Annual Reuters Trust Women "Stop Slavery Corporate" and "Personal Hero" awards.

Comparing our Contributions

Care points allow us to compare our contributions with others. Since the amount of points a person receives is visible to everyone using the app, we can see how we measure up to others. When this tool was tested in Hong Kong, it led to some friendly competitions between students and schools.

> *"When I saw that some of my friends had more points than I had, I decided to do more things. I wanted my work to be equal to theirs."*

Setting a Target

The *End Slavery App* allows users to set targets. I often suggest that students set a goal of at least 30 points. To achieve this target, the following activities could be done (among others).

- Read a book on the subject (2 care points)
- Watch a video on the topic (2 care points)
- Donate 20 hours of your time (8 care points)
- Donate $200 (16 care points)
- Listen to a podcast on the topic (2 care points)

Looking at the various categories and sub-categories listed on the app, a person's efforts can be tailored to their own experience, interest and desires. This flexibility is essential.

As the care point concept is expanded to include other issues, similar point systems and targets can be operationalized. This process has started in several cities in Asia. For example, the Sustainability Development Goals identified by the United Nations could be general categories. A participant picks a category and is then offered a series of actions they can take to gain points. Perhaps the number of points offered for learning could be standardized across all categories.

Standardizing Care Points

When I was applying for colleges 40 years ago, I had to fill out a different form for each college. When my sons went through the same process a few years ago, they filled out one basic form that could be used for all of the schools to which they applied. This standardization makes things so much easier for the schools and the students applying.

What if the care point system was standardized so that when applying for a university or a new job, a person could list the total number of care points they acquired over a given period of time? For this to happen, a system would need to be put in place to track and validate care point data.

One suggestion is to have a wiki-type voluntary community that standardizes the points and tracks and validates the supporting material. Since it would be too complicated to track every entry, an honor system could be used to cover a portion of the entries audited. This would reduce the number of people cheating with their points.

Offering Credits

At the end of each movie, every person who worked on the production is given a credit line. I recently stopped to read these credits on a film and saw designations like "Back-Up Painter" and "Coffee Assistant". This recognition is important to each and every one of the people listed. Many consider it a great honor.

What if we could come up with a comprehensive list of all those people who carried out heroic acts? This could easily be done using the care points system. Many people would sign up. The list would allow them to see how much service they gave compared to others. Just seeing all of the names would provide a sense of community. It would demonstrate that many people cared about helping to address the world's problems. It would be an inspiration to us all.

Care Currency

Several corporations have said they would consider offering gifts or incentives for people who earn certain amounts of care points. For example, if a person could show they received 100 care points, they might get a T-shirt or a free take out coffee. The idea would be to create a range of complementary incentives to get more and more people to participate.

The model for this is similar to airline frequent flyer points, which are tracked and accumulated with each flight taken and then redeemed for free flights or other awards. The systems and procedures to track millions of people are already developed. They could be easily adapted to track care points.

Imagine if we could all be rewarded for our good deeds. It would be a currency for good, based on good.

Care Communities

The care points concept could be scaled up to track the contributions of entire communities. For example, if a given town were to acquire 20,000 care points from their citizens, they could get a federal grant or some kind of program benefit. Many interesting, innovative approaches could be used to measure the outcome.

What is the Point?

We should consider tracking our heroic contributions. They have value and should be recognized and perhaps rewarded. By doing this, we would be able to build upon these ideas and concepts to explore innovative ways for care points and care currency to encourage participation in civic programs and activities.

One way to do this would be to encourage schools, universities, corporations, faith-based groups and the general public to offer suggestions on how to use, refine and adapt this concept.

It is time for us to celebrate our good actions. It is time to develop a standardized approach to measure them. It is time for us to value our collective "good".

14

SIMPLE ACTS OF HEROISM

This is YOUR chapter. I asked a handful of average people to explain their heroic moments. From these testimonials, you can see that everyone has their own story.

Damien, 20-year-old Veterinarian Student

For the past ten years, I have known that I wanted to spend my life working with animals. While in school, I have taken on several different opportunities as a way of exposing myself to different forms of animal care, to cultivate my understanding of animal welfare and to try to discover what it means to devote your life to the care of animals and their owners.

I'm currently volunteering with a turtle rescue team at the veterinary campus of my university. We shelter and rehabilitate mainly turtles and other reptiles that have been injured or are suffering from an illness and would not be able to survive on their own in the wild. Currently we care for approximately 80 turtles, giving them a safe and clean enclosure, as well as proper medication, to ensure that they are on the road to recovery. This program is helping to give these turtles a second chance at life and to allow them to be returned to their natural habitats where they belong.

These organizations show that people truly care about the natural world and the animals that live within our ecosystems. I have met so many enthusiastic volunteers and students that are all passionate about the proper care and welfare of these frail animals that are in need of our help. In finding this organization, I've found that there are numerous people who are willing to dedicate a substantial amount of time and energy towards the welfare of animals in need, which has helped to further cement my desire to continue along this path, knowing that I will meet more people like them in the future.

David, 43-year-old Finance Professional

A typical mid-week night out in town with colleagues led to a chance encounter and an unexpected opportunity to help someone in need.

The usual lively bar full of slightly drunk party people singing along with the band had one noticeable exception that night - a young girl standing on her own looking a bit unsure of herself.

We started talking. She explained how she'd been tricked into coming to Hong Kong with the promise of a safe waitressing job but instead had been given a huge debt to pay off before she would be allowed to return home to her family. With no other viable source of income, her only option was to start working the streets.

She'd never been to Hong Kong before, didn't know anyone and certainly hadn't previously been involved in any form of prostitution.

That first night, the best thing I could offer was friendship, genuine care and support, which I was more than happy to give to someone so clearly in need of help.

As I got to know her over the following few days and heard more of her story, I was inspired by her strength to deal with the crazy situation she found herself in. She was determined to keep going and not give up hope of getting back home as soon as she could.

We realized we needed to act quickly. She'd been "lucky" to have only been in Hong Kong for a few days. She hadn't gone with any clients and wasn't subjected to any violence by her captors. We wanted to keep things that way.

After searching the Internet, speaking to Hong Kong modern slavery support groups and checking with girls in similar situations, it soon became apparent that few options were available to her. The most effective was conceding to the demands of the people holding her and buying back her freedom.

This was my opportunity to make a truly great difference to someone's life. I didn't hesitate for a moment in gifting her the money to pay off her debt and get her life back.

Our plan worked. The sense of relief that we both shared was immense, especially when she sent me a video message when she was back at her home with her daughter.

Edward, 18-year-old High School Student

When I was younger, I used to participate in a charity event with my family. A group would go to the rural Shanxi state in China to teach English to children in a particular school. They were mainly kids from the neighboring villages who were subsidized by the charity to attend the school and we were tasked with preparing English lessons for them. Many of the volunteers spoke Cantonese and rarely used English but their sheer persistence and devotion in preparing quality lessons brought out their desire to give these children the best experience possible. They were not familiar with many of the terms themselves but they strived to learn them, working for hours on end to make the lessons entertaining and fruitful for the children, who in turn rewarded them with their inexhaustible excitement and energy.

It was great to see and participate in these connections between people of different cultures, especially in a time when tensions were high between China and Hong Kong. I was not familiar with politics back then but none of the volunteers seemed hindered by their cultural barriers in any way and gave their all for these kids.

Even though I no longer go to these events, I'm grateful for these opportunities to have witnessed unconditional human kindness, where the only aim was to see these kids happy and eager to pursue learning.

Arielle, 37-year-old NGO Volunteer

Hero seems to be a big word but to me, a common attribute to be deemed heroic would be to possess courage. Looking back at some of my short-term voluntary work – feeding the homeless at the notorious "Skid Row" district in Los Angeles, helping a media team to secretly film a documentary on child prostitution in Thailand, taking care of abandoned babies born with birth defects in Shanghai and simply the raising of my hand to be an ad hoc volunteer with an NGO countering online child pornography – I have come to realize it is not just about putting aside my time and resources but essentially bringing myself to face the difficult issues around me and further processing them within me.

It is always easier to walk away or turn a blind eye from something that tugs our hearts but your decision to say, "*Yes! I shall try to do something about this no matter how big or how small the impact may be,*" could just be your next courageous act to make this world a better place. In the words of C.S. Lewis, "*Courage is not simply one of the virtues but the form of every virtue at the testing point.*" Perhaps we can all be heroes in whichever space you feel compelled to act, to help and to love.

Zino, 36-year-old Singer/Songwriter

Before the unexpected opportunity of writing a song on the topic of human trafficking, I'd never understood what it was about or how the industry worked, let alone how many people were involved. Upon researching and listening to testimonies and talks about it, especially a real-life story about a girl called Gita, I started understanding that whatever we do, however small a task it may seem to us, to Gita, it could've meant an entirely different world.

Since my first involvement through music, I've been involved with hosting seminars across the city and raising awareness about human trafficking. It also sparked an interest for me to personally visit the country where Gita was from and to see her home. I've returned multiple times to visit victims living in a shelter dedicated to saving girls from human trafficking, some of them as young as five years old. It was difficult to gain their trust at first but through many visits and continued involvement in their welfare and health, some of them have accepted me as a friend; they even gave me a surprise birthday present.

Saying goodbye for the first time was like what you'd expect, a stranger's goodbye that was staged. However, as our relationship grew, each time was more passionate, more personal. *"Come back soon!"* yelled one of the girls. Our goodbyes became *"see you next time"*.

Small gestures, simple actions. Just like how I would treat any other human being. Because they are just that, the same as us, human beings. We don't need elaborate visits or involvement, or make a big commitment to live in another country. In an interview with a girl from a rural village whose friend had just died from human trafficking a day before we arrived, she said, *"We are just like you."* They don't have a voice, no one can hear them; Gita didn't have a voice but maybe you and I can simply become their voices. A small gesture, a simple action.

Mukeh, 29-year-old Filmmaker

When I was around nine years old, I happened upon a TV documentary that was about the lives of lepers in India. It was the first time the disease was depicted to me and my eyes were glued to the TV the moment I realized what they were talking about. While there was definitely a lot I empathized with, what got to me most wasn't the fact that there were people suffering from the disease. What got to me was how they explained that leprosy is curable and the people suffering from it didn't even know they could be cured. It was a disturbing reality that I have never gotten over.

I cried and went to the kitchen almost yelling at my mother, "*Why isn't anyone telling them that they can be cured? How can this happen?*" Even if the society that cast them out didn't know that there was a cure, it was unforgivable that another human being could be treated this way.

For me, social justice starts when we let someone suffering and vulnerable know that, "*I see you and I am fighting for you!*" I am developing certain skills with video and technology so that I can contribute to catalyzing people into becoming more tolerant, in the true sense of the word and being truly and unconditionally kind.

Susan, 44-year-old Cancer Service Volunteer

A frail, petite Indonesian woman with brain cancer came to see us one day. Her name was Lina. There was a heavy sadness about her, like a burial shroud of hopelessness. My heart immediately felt her despair and pain. She told us she was a domestic helper. The most marginalized people in Hong Kong are migrant women working as domestic helpers. They're considered second-class citizens.

A few weeks after surgery to remove part of her tumor, her employer, a bank manager, fired her. In Hong Kong, it's illegal to fire a helper while she's sick. This employer forced her to sign a resignation letter under duress.

Lina asked us for help. She had nowhere else to turn. Because she no longer had a work visa, she had to pay her own out-of-pocket expenses for her cancer treatment and consultation fees at the public hospital. This was eating into her meager life savings. Again, my heart went out to her.

To be honest, I am not a frontline worker or social worker type and I wasn't sure I could help her. I also wondered if this would take up a lot of my time and there was a moment of weighing up the cost and sacrifice. But I couldn't turn away from Lina's hollow eyes and skinny frame. I began to take little steps and typed out Lina's story and wrote an appeal. I shared her financial needs and that she needed a new employer to be able to stay in Hong Kong with a secure work visa. I sent out texts on WhatsApp to friends, asking them to help support Lina. I pondered for a few days over who could help. I had already exhausted my network of friends for help in my justice work.

A friend offered to donate HK$6,000 that day. A few days later, a woman's name came to mind. Jo was a dynamic Indonesian Chinese corporate lawyer. I asked her to consider helping Lina. Jo went even a few steps further by telling me that she was willing to hire Lina! I couldn't believe it! I connected Lina with other activists who could help advise her on dealing with the Immigration Department. Jo asked an employment agency to assist Lina in applying for her new work visa.

A small but powerful group of caring people came together to support Lina in her darkest hour. She was still having daily radiation therapy and chemotherapy at 3pm, yet she had to go to the Immigration offices to apply in person.

Having cancer did not give Lina a break but the power of kindness and compassion made a profound difference in her life. I also have more confidence in helping others – all it takes is a simple ask and forward motion.

Brandon, 22-year-old Medical Student

One experience I remember vividly occurred during a Habitat project in Nepal. My scout troop and I were visiting a small rural village, occupied by people in the lowest castes of the country's social hierarchy. We were divided and assigned various tasks throughout the village. My friends and I got the opportunity to renovate the small home of an elderly man.

He had spent his entire life in a small clay hut – roughly the size of a hotel room – without any electricity or running water and no furniture apart from a single bed. He was a farmer and shared this space with his goats and chickens. For many years he had been prohibited from building a second story to his house, as a result of his social class. After finally obtaining permission to do so after decades, we were tasked with building a second story over the next two days.

We worked diligently with local people and made substantial progress during the first day but the memorable part came at the day's end.

The elderly man started crying as he thanked us for our work, anticipating our return to finish the next day. Our translator told us that while he was excited to finally have more space of his own, what really touched him was the fact that several of us from around the world were taking time out of our lives to help him fulfill his wish. He was overwhelmed to discover that there were people out in the world that cared about him and others in his situation. In our two days with him we were able to show him that, despite the tribulations of his early life, the world hadn't forgotten about him.

Next Steps

This chapter has yet to be finalized. Please feel free to send me your own personal testimonial describing your heroic journey (300 words) to; matt.friedman@themekongclub.org. When the next edition of my book comes out, I will include a collection of additional vignettes.